100
Ways to Happiness
A guide for busy people

DR TIMOTHY J. SHARP

PENGUIN BOOKS

PENGUIN BOOKS

Published by the Penguin Group
Penguin Group (Australia)
250 Camberwell Road, Camberwell, Victoria 3124, Australia
(a division of Pearson Australia Group Pty Ltd)
Penguin Group (USA) Inc.
375 Hudson Street, New York, New York 10014, USA
Penguin Group (Canada)
90 Eglinton Avenue East, Suite 700, Toronto, Canada ON M4P 2Y3
(a division of Pearson Penguin Canada Inc.)
Penguin Books Ltd
80 Strand, London WC2R 0RL, England
Penguin Ireland
25 St Stephen's Green, Dublin 2, Ireland
(a division of Penguin Books Ltd)
Penguin Books India Pvt Ltd
11 Community Centre, Panchsheel Park, New Delhi – 110 017, India
Penguin Group (NZ)
67 Apollo Drive, Rosedale, North Shore 0632, New Zealand
(a division of Pearson New Zealand Ltd)
Penguin Books (South Africa) (Pty) Ltd
24 Sturdee Avenue, Rosebank, Johannesburg 2196, South Africa

Penguin Books Ltd, Registered Offices: 80 Strand, London, WC2R 0RL, England

10 9 8 7 6 5 4 3 2

Text copyright © Timothy J. Sharp 2008

Design by Danie Pout © Penguin Group (Australia)
Typeset in 9/15 The Sans by Sunset Digital, Brisbane, Queensland
Printed and bound in Australia by McPhersons Printing Group, Maryborough, Victoria

National Library of Australia
Cataloguing-in-Publication data:

Sharp, Timothy J.
100 ways to happiness: a guide for busy people / Dr Timothy J. Sharp.
9780143009030 (pbk.)
Includes index.
Happiness. Self-actualization (Psychology). Conduct of life.

158.1

penguin.com.au

This book is dedicated to my lovely and loving family; my wonderful wife, Marnie, and my inspirational children, Tali and Coby. To all three of you, I hope the many hours spent writing this book have in no way meant that I've been too busy to be a good husband and father!

Contents

Introduction

Many people are surprised to learn that these days the study of happiness is practically a science. How did this happen? Isn't happiness something that just 'is', something that comes and goes fairly randomly or that is experienced by just the lucky few? So how can we capture happiness, measure it and analyse it in the way that science requires?

For most of its history, the study of psychology has been concerned with what's *wrong* with people: the many social, emotional and physical dysfunctions that are all part of the human condition. Positive psychology, the name given to the study of happiness, is about how to maximise what's *right* – in other words, looking at what's working, why it's working and how to make it work even better.

Positive psychology emerged from the study of learned helplessness, depression and resilience: trying to understand the way in which some people, when faced with a challenge, will give up very easily, while others will persevere. Researchers identified that an optimistic outlook (among other things) is a key factor in a person's ability to keep on going in all sorts of situations, from completing a difficult task at work to surviving a major life setback. This may sound like bad news for those of us with a natural inclination towards pessimism, but there is good news: *we can learn to become more optimistic*, and, in the process, our happiness levels will increase. But how do we do this?

Much has been written on happiness in recent years, and a lot of it is fascinating stuff. However, it can also be quite academic and heavy-going, and most of us just don't have the time. This book has been written to bridge the gap between the very exciting developments in positive psychology and the general reader – the person who wants to tap in to the whole happiness thing without having to devote their life to the cause.

As well as being a coaching and consulting psychologist, I run conferences on happiness and speak at seminars. There is a burgeoning interest in these events; people are keen to learn about happiness and excited to hear that it is an achievable goal and not some vague state dependent on circumstances largely outside their control. They start to see how happiness can become a habit, like meditation or a daily walk. And they may even dip into some of the literature available to learn more. However, I can't count the number of times people have said to me, 'I want to be happy, but I just don't have the time.' They worry that they have to go through some complicated process to get there: spend years with a therapist; leave their wife; become New-age; change careers. Or they think they have to understand happiness from the inside out – to be in touch with all the research, know how it works, why it works.

My response to this is to compare happiness to technology. Technology is part of our everyday life. We drive our cars to work, heat our food in a microwave and send emails on our computer. We are extremely competent in these tasks, yet few of us know exactly how these devices work, and most of us don't have the time to find out. Likewise, we can 'practice' happiness and, in the process, become happier, without actually having to understand the mechanics of it. If you have never heard even a whisper about the benefits of positive psychology, you can pick up this book, flick to a page, and read about a simple exercise or practice that will help elevate your happiness levels.

I'm not saying that a deeper insight is not an incredibly useful thing. Some of you will choose to read this book cover to cover, and possibly go on to read other books on the subject (see Recommended Resources, page 166). We all know that the more we understand about a subject, the more we immerse ourselves in it and the more we can potentially gain from it. But at the same time, achieving happiness need not be overly complicated. There's no reason why we can't simply put the strategies here into practice, realise the benefits and enjoy our lives more, while finding the time for reflection and contemplation further down the track.

A minimum requirement for increasing one's happiness levels is a little bit of discipline. In Section One, '20 ways to happy habits', I talk about how it takes four weeks, on average, to establish a new habit. There is nothing mystical about this process; it is simply how our brains work (we need to lay down new neural and behavioural 'pathways' in order to establish new ways of doing things). In other words, unless you practise often and regularly, you won't get the benefit. The good news is that many of the practices suggested in this book can be slotted easily into your daily life. Some are as simple as:

- Making a list of things to be grateful for
- Practising a random act of kindness
- Challenging negative thoughts whenever they arise
- Warding off stress (the enemy of happiness) with some relaxation breathing
- Spending time with a person in your life who you regard as being positive.

You don't have to practise the same activity over and over – in fact, you will benefit from swapping things around, from alternating a 'happy-habit' practice with a 'happy-relationship' practice. It's rather like doing different sorts of exercise: swimming will help build your back and shoulder muscles; running will develop your leg muscles; Pilates will strengthen the muscles in your torso. And all three will combine to create a healthier, fitter you.

As with any work or household task, improving your happiness levels will require some thought and commitment to the task. But just by setting aside as little as ten minutes a day for happiness tasks – about the time it takes to watch the commercials in the average half-hour of television – you'll notice a difference. And while even this might seem a lot of time in a very busy life, once you start to see the benefits, there'll be no turning back.

Section One

20 ways to happy habits

We have been taught that happiness 'happens' when something good occurs; we all know how to recognise it, but we've neglected to learn how to prime ourselves for happy feelings and rather, tend to just wait for them to come to us. For example, the concept of practising healthy eating habits and working toward better fitness is familiar to all of us, yet we rarely put the same effort into creating happiness-building habits. Positive psychology is, at least in part, about taking a proactive approach to creating happiness rather than just waiting for it to happen; it's also about finding out and building on what already works rather than just fixing what's broken. Though habits take time to develop, you will, with some effort and discipline, find happiness is easy to achieve if you employ the following strategies. Being happy, as you will see, is as simple as brushing your teeth!

1. Redefine happiness

Beginning in childhood, we take our understanding of happiness for granted. 'Happy' and 'sad' are the first emotions we learn to recognise and express, and many of us haven't allowed this black-and-white definition to evolve as our lives and intellect have grown more complex – yet the more limited your definition of happiness is, the more difficult you will find it is to achieve.

Happiness, for me, is a term that covers a range of positive emotions. Ultimately, it means different things to different people – it's an entirely subjective experience. For some, the experience of happiness is one of predominately 'high arousal' feelings such as joy and excitement; for others, it involves more 'low arousal', but equally important, emotions such as calmness, contentment, peace and tranquillity.

Ideally, we should try to experience and enjoy all these different forms of positive emotions, but in all likelihood people who are more extroverted will tend more toward the high arousal end of the spectrum, while their more introverted counterparts will be more likely to seek out low arousal forms of happiness. Recognise that what makes you happy will differ from what makes someone else happy, and you will best spend your time expanding on things that work for you.

Take a pen and paper and list as many descriptions of positive emotion as you can think of. These need not be full sentences, but can simply be ideas or images that capture happiness in a new light. Be sure to add to this list whenever you think of additional positive emotions or colours within the happiness spectrum, remembering that happiness is an ever-expansive phenomenon.

I don't believe that anyone will be 100 per cent happy, 100 per cent of the time. True happiness involves recognising that as humans it's perfectly normal to experience the full range of emotions, including so-called 'negative' ones such as depression, anger, sadness, anxiety and stress. But by broadening your definition of happiness you can increase your opportunities to experience the full spectrum of positive emotions, and experience happiness more often.

2. Don't limit your potential

A client I once worked with grew up in the country and shared with me the following story:

> My father tended to and raised a beautiful vegetable garden and we would sell the produce at a small roadside stand we'd built ourselves. My parents always bought their chickens from a neighbour named Willy Scott.
>
> One day, when we were all out working at the vegetable stand, Willy delivered some chickens to the house in a crate and left them on the front patio. When we returned home later that day we discovered that the chickens had escaped and were running all over the yard. Everyone in the family began chasing the chickens and putting them back in the crate.
>
> My father was upset and decided to call Willy to express his unhappiness with the situation. He told him that he didn't think it was such a good idea to leave the chickens in a crate unattended, and how the family had had to chase chickens all around the neighbourhood; finally, he noted that they'd only been able to round up eleven. And then Willy provided a bit of a shock.
>
> 'Eleven chickens isn't too bad,' he exclaimed, 'I only delivered six!'

How much could each of us accomplish if we had no idea what the limits were? The potential each of us possesses is often restricted by our own self-imposed limits. Recognising these is the first step toward overcoming them.

Are you listless at work? Perhaps it is time to ask for more responsibility. Do you enjoy writing poetry in your spare time? Perhaps it is time to enter it in a competition or take it to a writers' group. Have you competed in a few 5 km fun runs? Perhaps it is time to try a longer race. Work outside your comfort zone, and next time *you* might find eleven chickens when you thought there were only six!

3. Reduce the 'shoulds'

A lot of unhappy people continue doing what they are doing even though they know it is the cause of their unhappiness.

Much of this habitual behaviour stems from one small word – 'should'. Every single one of us has responsibilities we must maintain and, in fact, a great deal of our genuine happiness in life comes from honouring commitments to family, work and community. However, all of us at some time must contend with a series of extraneous 'shoulds' – those pressing concerns that, in the bigger scheme of things, might not be that important after all.

These are the voices we carry from childhood: 'You "should" polish your shoes every day' or 'You "should" never put saucepans in the dishwasher'. Often these are not our own rules, they are someone else's – our mother's, teacher's, cousin's, or the next-door neighbour's. And although they may be sound rules, they can also make unnecessary claims on our time and energy, preventing us from doing the things that make us happy.

For example, washing the kitchen floor three times a week, when once will do, might stop you from taking a calming walk. Jumping up to do the dishes as soon as the meal is finished will mean you can't join in the family conversation, just as it's getting interesting. And working assiduously through your lunch break could prevent you from enjoying the sort of interaction with colleagues that can make a work environment a more pleasant place to be.

Make a list of all the 'shoulds' in your life. Have a think about when you first started to regard an activity as a 'should', and who encouraged this. Then put a line through any 'shoulds' that are no longer working for you – those that are now well past their expiry date. Make a point of resisting the 'shoulds' whenever they pop up. Sit longer at the dinner table; drag yourself away from the computer screen. In doing so, you will start to create new patterns that better suit your life and interests in the here and now.

> *Let the world know you as you are, not as you think you should be, because sooner or later, if you are posing, you will forget the pose, and then where are you?*
>
> Fanny Brice, 1891–1951, American comedienne

4. Have a 'happy hour'

Most of us have heard of the term 'happy hour', one often used by pubs and clubs when they are selling drinks cheap for a period of time. In truth, alcohol is a depressant and certainly not good for your happiness.

My definition of a happy hour is spending 60 minutes engaging in any activity which you find pleasurable and satisfying. There is no need to wait for a special occasion to enjoy yourself. Compile a list of happiness-inducing activities and start planning them into your schedule on a regular basis. Make sure you treat them with the same importance as you would a meeting with your boss or an appointment with your most important client.

Even, and especially during, particularly busy times make sure to find time (preferably at least a few minutes every day, with no distractions) which you can spend on your own in a quiet and peaceful place. Concentrate on relaxing, reflecting on your thoughts and feelings, and reviewing the day past and the days to come. Use this time to learn more about yourself and prepare in a positive way.

Practise incorporating this recreational time into your life and you will soon see that you don't need to wait for Friday afternoon to have a happy hour!

5. Practise incremental change

We all appreciate that you cannot build something the scale of the Sydney Harbour Bridge overnight, yet people often become frustrated or impatient when they cannot achieve great change in their own lives right away. I encourage you to consider that the best way to achieve massive and meaningful life changes – ones that will lead you to experience and enjoy a truly happy and fulfilled life – is to plan to make lots of small changes on a regular basis. For those of you who like formulas, I have composed an equation to show this:

(Small changes) x (regular application) = big change!

In other words, you don't have to change your life all in one day. If you regularly make small, positive changes you will eventually experience significant life-changing benefits. Creating new habits takes a minimum of four weeks, and requires repetition and dedication on your part.

It is also daunting to contemplate making large changes all at once, and you are far more likely to achieve your goals through making small adjustments on a regular basis.

Take one thing in your life that you would like to change, and break it down into small increments of change that can fit into your existing schedule. Stick with your plan to change something for good, and remember that it takes a while to make the foundations before you can start building the bridge. Just because you can't see the results doesn't mean you aren't effecting change.

6. Alter bad habits

Most people know what they should do to live a healthier and happier life. To be fitter and healthier, for example, everyone knows they should eat less fat, sugar and salt, eat more fruit and vegetables and exercise more. Recognising the changes we have to make is not rocket science. So why do so few people do these things well?

The reason is that few people have an effective system in place to achieve change. If you want to develop healthier habits you are far better equipped to succeed if you use a strategy.

Rather than embarking on a regime which aims simply to do away with bad habits, you need a system which at the same time replaces these with new, helpful habits. You will be far more likely to eliminate existing bad habits if you substitute them with positive habits – much in the same way that people who are overweight often have more success losing weight if they substitute undesirable foods with healthier foods, rather than just not eating.

Identify when it is you typically engage in a negative behaviour, and put in place a plan to alter this behaviour in that setting. For example, if you find that your healthy eating plan tends to fail when you eat out at restaurants, find out about the menu before you go, and make a healthy choice in advance. Habits are built into our routine, and often we don't consciously think about engaging in certain sorts of behaviour. Once you single out the circumstances in which you are most likely to revert to 'old' behaviour, you are able to plan to prevent it.

Reward yourself for making positive changes, and for trying to engage in healthy and productive activities. Remember that even if you are only successful half of the time, you are still training yourself for the future.

Celebrating your efforts will significantly increase your chances of continuing helpful habits in the long term.

Small opportunities are often the beginning of great enterprises.
Demosthenes, 384–322 BC, Greek statesman

7. Spring-clean your life – regularly

We've all heard the phrase 'cluttered desk, cluttered mind', and there is a very real benefit to organising the chaos from a psychological point of view. Many of you would already be very familiar with the sense of satisfaction we experience following an annual spring-clean. As cathartic as this overhaul is though, you are missing out on opportunities to replicate this harmony throughout the year!

Tidying up our mess and cleaning out our cupboards are healthy habits in both a literal and metaphorical sense, and things we should do on a regular basis. Start by getting rid of belongings that you do not need and avoid the urge to hold on to things for sentimental reasons. Though keepsakes can be a fantastic trigger for happy thoughts, hoarding things from the past keeps you from looking forwards to your future. The same goes for recurring thoughts, grudges or regrets: make a point of letting things go from time to time.

Reorganising your house can help you to establish new routines, and break the monotony of daily life. For example, sorting through your closet will help you to dispose of old or unflattering clothes, saving you time and leaving you with garments that make you feel good. Placing your work-out clothes where they are more accessible can encourage exercise.

If a job is too big then simply break it down into smaller, more manageable chunks. Happiness accumulates a bit like compound interest – a little effort today will go a long way tomorrow.

Finally, don't wait until September to spring-clean: tidy your home and your life as often as you need to. Get rid of physical and psychological rubbish at regular intervals and enjoy the positive consequences. You will find that freedom, happiness and a sense of relief follow.

8. Get it done today

Avoidance is a common way of dealing with problems: we've all done it before and we'll all do it again in the future. Avoidance means not facing up to something that's bothering us or denying the reality of a situation. The problem with such an approach to life's changes is that it works quite well in the short term, but only in the short term.

When we have unresolved issues, we experience an emotional disquiet which can be significantly stressful, so if something's not right or if something's troubling you, do something about it.

Often what keeps us from attending to a problem is a fear of the unknown. Avoiding a doctor's visit not only leaves our ailments untreated, but permits our worries to run wild. Identify the tasks you have been putting off, and work out why it is you are delaying something important. Acting may not always alter the circumstances, but denial is an emphatically futile and ineffective coping mechanism; by acting positively you increase the chances of a positive outcome (sometimes in spite of the situation). Sorting through your problems is actually very beneficial, and can contribute to feelings of satisfaction, contentment and happiness.

So don't procrastinate! If something needs to be done, just do it. The longer you put it off, the longer you'll feel frustrated and disgruntled. But as soon as you get stuck in and do what you need to do, you'll almost certainly experience positive emotions such as happiness, pride and satisfaction.

9. Look at your upbringing objectively

Our thoughts (those vitally important things that essentially determine whether or how we experience happiness) don't just pop out of thin air, but rather evolve out of deeper, underlying beliefs, or what psychologists often refer to as schema. In simple terms, these deeper beliefs are similar to those more accessible, 'surface-level' thoughts but differ in the sense that they tend to be about bigger, more global issues rather than the specifics of what's happening right here and now.

So, if someone says something to you that you find offensive, insulting or upsetting in some way, you might react with 'automatic thoughts' about that person, what they said and what it meant to you. These thoughts would have arisen out of the deeper beliefs you'd developed over the years about people in general and whether, for example, they're inherently good or bad.

Without overcomplicating things, these beliefs, expectations and assumptions that we have tend to cover issues such as your attitudes towards yourself (as a person and your position in the world), others (and what they're like and what their intentions typically are) and the world (as a place in which to exist). Core beliefs like this typically evolve in early childhood, which means the most influential shapers of these beliefs are our parents. Looking objectively at the influence your parents had on you can be liberating and insightful (though blaming them for all your foibles will be of only limited productivity).

So ask yourself:

- What did my parents tell me about the world?
- What did my parents think of other people?

- How did my parents describe and view me? (Was, for example, my parents' perception of me shaped by my position in the family?)
- Were my parents' views coloured in any way by religious or cultural (or even generational) beliefs?
- Just because my parents believed this, does that mean I should?

The rationale for asking such questions lies in the fact that many of us hold on to beliefs and engage in habitual behaviours simply because that's what our parents or relatives or teachers did or told us to do.

Now I'm not for one minute suggesting that everything your mother or father or grandparents said or did was wrong, but I am suggesting it's worth considering whether everything they did or said was right; and even if it was right for them at that time, is it necessarily helpful for you now?

Ultimately, there are no thoughts or ways of thinking that are perfect. Rather, what you should be aiming for are thoughts that work for you, given your situation, at this point in time.

When faced with a situation where your beliefs conflict with the behaviour of others, you can either effect change in others, or alter your beliefs. Allow yourself the latitude to determine your own ethical framework: being open-minded is a wonderful way to reduce your conflict with the world around you.

When we are no longer able to change a situation,
we are challenged to change ourselves.
Viktor Frankl, 1905–1997, Austrian neurologist and psychiatrist

10. Forgive others

No matter who you are, there is no doubt that at some point in your life someone will do you wrong. They will upset you, betray you, or engage in some form of behaviour that you consider to be inappropriate.

Although it's perfectly normal to experience these feelings, it isn't healthy to allow these emotions to take over your life or to impact on your functioning for a prolonged period. The ability to forgive others is an important part of happiness. If you refuse to forgive, you are perpetuating the time you spend as the victim: for every minute you're bitter or angry you lose a minute when you could potentially be feeling happy!

The good news is that it is possible to practise forgiveness once you understand the full meaning of this word. Forgiveness is not simply forgetting what someone has done, condoning or excusing their actions, irrationally trusting their judgement, relinquishing your legal rights, or reconciling with someone where there is a danger to anyone's safety or health. In other words, forgiveness is conditional upon you preserving your rights and feelings.

Forgiveness is not a one-step process, and the bigger the infraction against you, the more difficult it may be. Is there a grudge you have been holding for too long? Do something about it!

Begin by fully acknowledging what has happened and the pain you have experienced. Decide exactly what forgiveness means within the specific context of your experience and in relation to the person in question – this may depend on the scale of the betrayal and the intent of the other party.

Make a real effort to understand the other person's position and what might have motivated them to do what they did that ultimately hurt you.

Where and whenever possible, allow yourself to empathise, even if only for the briefest of moments.

Look at the experience as a lesson and try to find some redemptive meaning within it. Is there any way that you can learn from, or see life as being richer for, the whole experience?

An important step in the forgiveness process is discussing all the relevant issues with the person or people involved. Let them know how you feel and avoid placing blame. You will find that forgiveness benefits both parties, and can actually act as a galvanising experience for a friendship or relationship.

> *Forgiveness does not change the past,*
> *but it does enlarge the future.*
> Paul Boese, 1668–1738, Dutch physician

11. Be your own guru

In certain Eastern spiritual traditions, teachers or 'wise men' are sometimes referred to as gurus. These are people to whom one can turn for guidance or advice.

If you have a guru in your life – a coach, mentor, counsellor or even just a good friend – then you're lucky, because it's wonderfully helpful to have someone like this to ask for assistance. But what if you don't have anyone? Or what if your guru is unavailable when you really need them?

What if you could be your own guru?

Ask yourself, what would my guru say? What would they advise? If you know someone – let's say their name is Jane – who always seems to have the right answer or question just when you need it, then ask yourself, 'What would Jane say?'

Keep track of helpful advice you have given others: often we feel comfortable directing other people yet feel overwhelmed in our own lives. Take a step back and look at the situation objectively – *you* may be the best person to advise yourself!

Learning to be self-sufficient will build your self-esteem, and taking responsibility for your own life means your successes are attributable only to you. Your experiences are as important as other's, and the sooner you learn to trust yourself, the more positive you will feel toward yourself and the level of control you have in your life.

12. Recognise your strengths

Carefully consider the following story:

> A water bearer in China had two large pots hung on the ends of a pole, which he carried across his neck. One of the pots had a crack in it, the other pot was perfect.
>
> At the end of the long walk from the stream to the house, the perfect pot would always be full of water, but the cracked pot would arrive only half full. For two years this went on every day, with the bearer delivering only one and a half pots of water to his house. Of course, the perfect pot was proud of its accomplishments. But the poor cracked pot was ashamed of its own imperfection, and miserable that it was able to accomplish only half of what it had been made to do.
>
> After two years of what it perceived to be bitter failure, the cracked pot spoke to the water bearer one day by the stream. 'I am ashamed of myself, because this crack in my side causes water to leak out all the way back to your house.'
>
> The bearer said to the pot, 'Did you notice that there are flowers on your side of the path, but not on the other pot's side? That's because I have always known about your flaw, so I planted flower seeds on your side of the path, and every day while we walk back, you water them. For two years I have been able to pick these beautiful flowers to decorate the table. Without you being just the way you are, there would not be this beauty to grace the house.'

Each of us has our own unique flaws, and it's these that make our lives together so very interesting and rewarding. You've just got to accept yourself for what you are and everyone else for what they are, and look for the good in all people.

To find out your strengths, ask yourself a series of questions:

- What switches you on?
- When do you feel most alive?
- When do you feel most yourself?
- Which new skills do you learn very easily?
- What do you look forward to?
- What do you look back on with fondness?

Try the following exercise. Get out your diary, calendar or whatever system you use to organise your life. Look at all the tasks, activities and appointments you have coming up in the next 2–4 weeks: which of these are you really looking forward to or are really excited about? Is there a common theme to these activities or tasks? If so, can you plan to have more of whatever this is in your life?

Look at all the tasks, activities and appointments you've completed or attended in the previous 2–4 weeks: which of these did you find enjoyable, energising, motivating or inspirational? Is there a common theme to these activities or tasks and if so, can you plan to have more of whatever this is in your life?

Put aside your modesty, at least for a few minutes, and write down all the things that you most value about yourself, your relationships and your work. The following list may help prompt you:

appreciation of beauty and excellence

being loved

bravery

caution

citizenship

critical thinking

curiosity

diligence

discretion

enthusiasm

equity

fairness

faith

forgiveness

generosity

gratitude

hope

humility

humour

industry

ingenuity

integrity

interest in the world

judgement

kindness

leadership

love of learning

loving

loyalty

mercy

modesty

open-mindedness

optimism

originality

passion

perseverance

perspective

playfulness

practical intelligence

prudence

self-control

sense of purpose

social and emotional intelligence

spirituality

teamwork

valour

The challenge for all of us wanting to experience more happiness is to find out what our talents are, and then go for broke in whatever area or life domain it happens to be. Engage in activities that flaunt your existing strengths, and avoid berating yourself for your weaknesses – there is always a flip-side to them!

13. Find flow

Flow (or what sports people might refer to as being 'in the zone') is that feeling you get when you're involved in something so deeply that nothing else seems to matter and you lose track of time. Flow activities are typically done for their own sake, because they're intrinsically rewarding. Where getting a massage would give us instant joy, flow activities tend to require our full attention and active involvement, and don't deliver instant gratification. They challenge our abilities and strengths just enough to be enjoyable, but not too much that we find them stressful (if we don't challenge ourselves or utilise our strengths often enough, we find we experience boredom). Some activities that induce flow could be cycling, rock climbing, playing music, playing bridge, completing crosswords or puzzles, practising yoga or meditation, writing or reading a book.

Simple pleasures like eating chocolate or having a hot shower diminish over time as our body gets used to the sensation. To achieve the same levels of enjoyment we need progressively more chocolate or more hot water. In comparison, complex tasks don't give out instant rewards, but will leave you with a much greater sense of achievement at the end.

In a society that puts an increasing premium on enjoyment we are often bombarded with opportunities for instant satisfaction. What is lost is the deeper sense of achievement gained through completing a more demanding task. Running a marathon is not inherently enjoyable while you are out pounding the pavement, your body wearying as the miles stretch on, but its positive effects of pride and triumph will last much longer than the excitement that, say, purchasing a new pair of shoes would bring.

Think about the last few times you experienced flow. When was the last time you completely lost track of time or 'zoned out' while completing a task? What were you doing and what strengths were you utilising?

When you next have some leisure time, choose a more demanding task over a simple pleasure, and note the after-effects. Make an effort to perform more of these tasks. Ask yourself how you can experience more flow, and don't always go for the easy fix.

> *Let me tell you the secret that has led me to my goal.*
> *My strength lies solely in my tenacity.*
> Louis Pasteur, 1822–1895, French chemist

14. Transfer your skills

Where do you shine at work – and how can you take this home? Where do you shine at home – and how can you take this to work?

One of the more interesting observations I've made over the years I've worked as a psychologist and coach is that in some cases people are not good at generalising or transferring certain behaviours from one situation to another.

I've seen and worked with people who are great parents, but not very good managers. At the same time I've seen people who are highly successful at work but unhappy in their personal lives.

It need not be like this, because the skills that lead to success in one area of our lives could just as easily lead to success (however we define this) in other areas. Happiness and success often come to those who are good at recognising where their strengths lie, and who are just as good at utilising these strengths in one domain as another.

Choose either your work life or home life, and identify your greatest strengths in that setting. Are you cool under pressure at the office? You might feel that you are 'boring' at home, when in fact your great skill is buffering conflict in the family. If you are loved at home for your humour and creativity, you might find that you actually have a knack for lateral thinking and generating drive at your workplace. If you are a 'people person' and thrive on planning barbeques on the weekend, make sure you are put in the way of clients and associates at work to best make the most of your skills. The key is finding ways to implement your strengths in all the facets of your life.

15. Keep focussed

In the next section, '20 ways to a happy body', I provide quite a few pointers on how to relax using meditation and other breathing techniques, skills that are really important for long-term calm and happiness. This is the fast-track version, a few quick tips to turn your attention – quickly – from your worries and regrets to more positive thoughts.

When we worry, we obsess about the future; when we experience regret, we fixate too much on the past. Letting our mind wander in either direction, to the point where we feel pain, prevents us from getting the most out of the present; we stop enjoying the moment and are less able to think of good solutions to problems or to look for ways to deepen our contacts with the people we love.

Develop a short phrase that you can say to yourself to pull you into the here and now. One of my editors told me that when she is faced with a particularly tricky or uncomfortable situation, she uses the age-old phrase: 'This too shall pass'. Such a saying serves as a little reminder; a gentle prod to shift our anxious or regretful thoughts. There are plenty of inspirational quotes from great thinkers that can serve this purpose – have a look on the internet, read biographies of inspiring people or refer to one of the many books of quotes that are around.

Another useful technique, particularly if you are quite a visual person, is to find an inspiring picture to pin above your desk, beside your bed or on the fridge. Get into the habit of looking at the picture whenever you start feeling your stress levels rise. Try also keeping a list of goals close by which will remind you of the bigger picture, or maybe a letter or email of appreciation from a friend or a work associate that highlights the good things others see in you.

16. Keep a positive events diary

A slightly more convenient version of the appreciation and gratitude exercises described in this section, the positive events diary emphasises the importance of listing and attending to good things that have happened in your life on each particular day.

Accordingly, it's best to do this later in the day, in the afternoon or early evening, and as with many of these exercises it's best to write these things down (not just think about them).

All you need is pen and paper, and all you need to do each night is to write down 3–5 good things that have happened that day. Some days this will be relatively easy; on other days, it might be a struggle, but it's these 'struggle' days when this exercise is even more important and will really provide a boost to your happiness and wellbeing.

You may like to simply list the people you met that day with whom you had a positive interaction. You could focus on the productive things you did, what it was you learnt or the moment that made you the happiest. The key is reinforcing the good each day has brought, and offsetting anything negative or untoward. Even if you take only one good thing from each day to record, you're ahead.

17. Practise gratitude exercises

Memory is inherently flawed. Your recollection of an event may be different your friend's; eyewitness testimony is frequently deemed inadmissible as there is no smooth process by which events become 'saved' in our minds. Some people, on looking back at their life, remember only the happy moments and perceive their life as very joyful; conversely, people who have spent more time focussing on their shortcomings will have managed to ingrain these moments in their memory, resulting in a more negative recollection of the past.

If you would rather view the world through rose-tinted glasses, you simply need to reinforce the positive moments you have experienced. One way to do this is to practise gratitude every night before you go to bed, or every morning as you wake and start the day (or both!) For example:

- List (preferably in writing) 3–5 things in your life for which you're grateful, and take some time to reflect on them.
- Meditate on anything and everything in the world you believe deserves to be appreciated.
- List the 5 most important people in your life. They could be the ones you love the most, the ones you see the most, or the ones who have the most impact on your life for whatever reason. Then, focussing on one person each night for the next week, specifically describe 5 things about each person that you feel appreciative of. If you complete this exercise, at the end of the week you'll have a list of 5 people with at least 5 'blessings' for each. That's 25 things for which you can be grateful, and I'm pretty confident that if you then sit back and reflect on this list, you'll feel happier.

- List all the various aspects of your job (or your home or other duties) for which you're thankful. This is, I think, a particularly useful exercise as many people tend to focus exclusively on the negative aspects of this part of their lives, despite the fact that it leads to great satisfaction and wellbeing. For example, I'm grateful for the fact I:

  - get paid to do something I love
  - help people in some way every day
  - work and interact with wonderful colleagues.

To multiply the effects of this simple but powerful exercise, share your thoughts and appreciations with someone close. A positive attitude is contagious and can actually make you more attractive to other people.

18. Make rest a priority

Two woodcutters head out to the forest for a day's work. The first woodcutter picks up his saw and goes as hard as he can, all day, not even stopping for a drink of water or for lunch, believing that as long as he keeps working hard, he'll chop more wood and, therefore, earn more money.

The second woodcutter also works hard but frequently takes breaks, and it seems to the first woodcutter that every time he glances over at his colleague the other man is resting, taking a drink of water or fiddling with his saw. Yet, despite this, his pile of wood always seems larger and higher than the first woodcutter's. How could this be?

After hours of persistent hard work, covered in sweat and close to exhaustion, the first woodcutter eventually takes a minute out of his labours and asks the other man how he has been able to chop so much wood when he seems to take so many breaks. The other cutter responds: 'That's simple. Every hour or so I stop and sharpen my saw. That way, my blade is more able to cut through the wood and the chopping is so much easier!'

This story illustrates the importance of regularly taking breaks to refresh, revitalise, rest and recuperate. Resting the body, mind and spirit is really taking time to 'sharpen the saw'. I have no doubt that this analogy is just as relevant for happiness, so if you feel your blade is becoming blunt (ie if you're feeling burnt-out, tired, listless or lacking motivation) then stop for a while, sharpen your saw and tend to your physical and mental energies.

Getting enough sleep is one of the best happiness habits you can form. We spend an estimated one-third of our lives sleeping, and it is vitally important in the recovery and restoration of our energy, yet the quality of our sleep is often below par. Many people do not sleep well because they simply aren't aware of the things they could do to help them sleep better. Other people are aware of what they should do but do not prioritise sleep because they believe other things are more important.

Once you begin to experience the benefits of sleep, hopefully it will be a priority forever. For now, at the very least, try to make it your main priority for a minimum of 4–6 weeks. Set yourself a sleep goal of 7 or 8 hours per night. To help with this, provide as many answers as you can to the questions below:

- Why am I sick of not sleeping?
- What can I gain (what will the benefits be) from sleeping better?

Remind yourself of these reasons as often as you need to. Make sleep non-negotiable! See page 47 for more details on how to establish a good sleep routine.

19. Create a rewards system

The exercises and strategies contained in this book are really a kind of training for your mind. Just as an athlete conditions their body to achieve a higher level of fitness, so you can finetune your body to achieve a high peak of positive emotion. We learn to repeat behaviour that brings gratification and it is important to acknowledge our successes so that we are motivated to repeat them.

Reward yourself when you practise the strategies or do the things you know are good for your mood and health. That is, give yourself a 'pat on the back'; actively tell yourself you've done a good thing.

Create a points system where you can earn points from healthy behaviour and reward yourself when you accumulate enough points in your system.

Rewards could also be more tangible but should be matched in size and significance to the size and significance of your efforts and achievements. Taking this into account, buy yourself some-thing special when you achieve something meaningful; plan a special activity (such as making your favourite dinner or soaking in a hot bath) for when you've successfully mastered a skill or completed a happiness-related task.

20. Remember to be happy!

Most of us brush our teeth at least once every day, and at around the same time.

Do you ever forget to brush your teeth?

I ask this question quite a lot, and I'm no longer surprised when I hear people answer 'no'. We very rarely forget to brush our teeth for one reason: we've developed a strong routine that makes it part of our lives – a part of our lives we can complete on 'automatic pilot'.

What if you practised happiness strategies in the same way you brush your teeth? What if you practised these strategies so routinely you never forgot them?

Once people have grasped the principles of positive psychology, which in reality is not that hard to do, the most common obstacles are not metaphysical, philosophical or anything really that complicated. People simply forget – they forget to practise the things they have discovered make them happy, and they even forget why happiness itself is so important in their lives.

As John Lennon once said, life's what happens to you while you're busy making other plans. Putting my own spin on this, I'd say happiness is what doesn't happen to you if you're too busy making other plans!

Much of what you'll read in this book is commonsense, but what I've learned in my many years of working with all sorts of individuals is that commonsense is not often common practice. So how can you remember to do all the great things positive psychology tells us to do?

Use reminders, just as you might to ensure you don't forget other important things. Reminders come in many shapes and sizes but some of the more practical ones include:

- Diary entries – write in your diary exactly what you want to do and exactly when you want to do it
- Post-it notes – write down key words and phrases, and stick them in places where you won't miss them (for example, on your computer, car steering-wheel or sun visor, your bedside table or the fridge)
- And for those of you who are more technologically adept, take advantage of the numerous electronic alarms and reminders that can be automatically scheduled.

> *The discipline of writing something down is the first step toward making it happen.*
> Lee Iacocca, 1924–1983, American industrialist

Section Two

20 ways to a happy body

Most of us recognise that the busy, corporate lifestyle of today takes its toll on the health of society in general. When our bodies are out of shape, functioning poorly and suffering the effects of stress, it is very hard for us to be happy. Those who put effort into exercising, treating their bodies kindly and taking the time to relax are training not only their physique but also their mind to function more efficiently and maximise its capacity for happiness.

21. Exercise now

I'm sure you're all well aware that exercising is a crucial component of healthy living. The last few decades have seen a huge amount of public education about activity and healthy living. The focus, however, has predominately been on telling people what's good for them, when in my opinion, most people already know! So this tip is not about describing the many benefits of activity and exercising, but rather suggesting some strategies that will make it more likely you'll exercise on a regular basis.

Commencing exercise can seem daunting to those who are out of the habit, but it is truly as simple as standing up and moving. It requires no preparation and no equipment, the important thing is to start now! Often the hardest part of exercise is getting out the door; once you are out you will probably find your motivation increases.

It doesn't matter what you do – any amount of activity is better than none. Learn to improvise wherever you are. If you enjoy indoor activities like Pilates, tai chi or yoga, and have no place to practise, find a grassy spot outside. If you can't afford weights, use unopened cans of food instead or perform resistance exercises (such as simple squats, push-ups and sit-ups) using your own body weight.

Your chances of continuing to exercise will be far greater if you engage in something you enjoy. There is no point dragging yourself out to the tennis club if you hate racquet sports! If you don't like doing freestyle swimming, stick to breast stroke or use a kickboard.

Mix up your activities. Running the same circuit over and over will tire you mentally; vary your route and you will maintain motivation. This is perhaps more important for those of you who work out in a gym – the surroundings don't change, so make a point of varying your workout. Opt for a cross-country course one day, and intervals the next. This technique has been used by athletes for years to optimise their training.

If you exercise with someone else, your enjoyment of an activity will be greatly increased, you will be more likely to follow through with it, and you will probably be distracted from your exertion. On days when your motivation is lacking, an exercise partner can help – competition drives us that little bit harder.

Think of yourself as an athlete: monitor your progress and achievements, and reward yourself for keeping active and exercising. Take yourself, and your exercising, seriously!

The biggest room in the world is the room for improvement.
Source unknown

22. Exercise to boost your mood

As good as exercise and activity are for your health, they're also wonderfully good for your mental health and psychological wellbeing. Exercise is a powerful anti-depressant as well as one of the quickest, simplest and most effective mood-enhancers. When we exert ourselves the brain releases endorphins – the same neuro-transmitters that give us a natural high when we fall in love.

I recommend you use exercise to both prevent and treat ill-health. Instead of reaching for the icecream when you feel blue, go for a walk, get your blood flowing and induce a natural happy mood. The benefits are two-fold: not only will you release endorphins to increase your happiness, you will also experience a sense of achievement later on for having done something good for your body.

So the next time you are feeling negative, stop and determine to do something active. Stretch, walk around the block, run up a steep hill or do some sit-ups; anything that gets your body moving!

The more you exercise, the more you'll find you crave exercise, thanks to the chain of neuro-chemical activity it induces. This means that exercising becomes progressively more attractive to you as you train, and as a result becomes habitual and self-reinforcing.

23. Practise mindful exercise

Mindfulness involves being intentionally aware of your thoughts and actions in the present moment, non-judgementally. It can be practised as part of any activity – for example, walking.

In its simplest form, mindful walking can be started by concentrating on your breathing and on the movement of your feet. Be sure to maintain a steady focus on these two things and do your best to refocus if you find yourself distracted. As you become more skilled you might like to try a slightly more complex version that involves taking notice of various elements for each step, such as the pushing, lifting, swinging and dropping of each foot.

Exercise physiologists have long understood that when weightlifters concentrate on their muscles as they lift a weight (in a mirror, for example), the exercise builds a greater muscle mass than would result from a lack of concentration. This same principle can be adapted to any activity you perform, in fact, mindfulness can be applied to almost any movement you make, and will not only increase your kinesthetic awareness (knowing where your body is in space) but also your body–mind connection.

24. Take a 'thank you' walk

Try to take a 'thank you' walk every morning or evening. This is different to walking for fitness, health, relaxation or even to enhance your mindfulness. It is about practising gratitude, and walking is a great way to clear and clarify the mind.

So while you're walking, running, riding or doing whatever form of exercise you most enjoy, talk to yourself (quietly and peacefully in the back of your mind) about all the things in your life for which you're thankful. You can direct your thanks to a god, if you believe in one, to a specific individual (including yourself if appropriate), or just generally to the world at large.

By doing this, you will maximise the effects of your exercise as well as intrinsically reward yourself for taking the time to be active.

> *I would maintain that thanks are the highest form of thought,*
> *and that gratitude is happiness doubled by wonder.*
> G.K. Chesterton, 1874–1936, English writer

25. Practise controlled breathing

Did you know that people who practise relaxation or meditation on a regular basis are healthier and live longer?

Relaxation techniques can be extremely useful. They can help you to more effectively manage stress, tension and anxiety. They can help you perform better at work and remain calmer in any situation. They can help you get to sleep (and fall asleep again if you wake during the night). They can be used at work or at home, on the bus or while you are standing in a queue. Relaxation is a skill that will become more effective and easier with practise; and your goal should be to master relaxation so that you can do it (pretty much) anywhere and anytime (ie not just lying down in your bed with the blinds down and the door closed!).

One method of relaxation is 'controlled breathing'. It is most effective in reducing anxiety and helping you to keep calm, and is quick and easy to practise wherever you are. Simply follow these instructions:

1. Make yourself as comfortable as you can, depending on where you're practising this (and again, don't just try this at home in a quiet room but rather, try to apply it in a range of situations, some easy and some more difficult).

2. Begin by breathing normally and don't make any effort to change your breathing in any way. Just let your body determine its own natural pace, but gradually focus your mind more and more on your breath.

3. Start paying attention to your breathing and to making it slow and even. Then, when you're ready, quietly start saying to yourself 'in' when you breathe in, and 'relax' when you breathe out. Repeat

this over and over again. Focus as much as you can on these
two simple words.

4. As you're breathing nice and slowly and repeating these two
   simple words, imagine that with every breath out, each time
   you say 'relax', you are becoming calmer and more relaxed. Just
   imagine that all the strains and stresses drain out of you with
   every exhalation and every repetition of the word 'relax'.
5. If you get distracted by any noises or if your thoughts wander (as
   they no doubt will) gently ease your mind back to your breathing
   and those two simple words, 'in' and 'relax'. Refocus as often as you
   need to.

Practise this as often as you can: as a general rule of thumb, I'd recommend
you try to do at least 3–5 practice sessions each day. Each session need
only be 3–5 minutes long (although it is worth trying to fit in at least one
longer session of about 10–15 minutes as well). As noted above, it's also
worth trying to practise in as many different situations as possible so you
can ultimately do it anywhere you need to.

Don't forget, practise is the key. If you can practise regularly you'll
gradually master the skill and begin to realise the benefits.

26. Practise progressive muscle relaxation

This method of relaxation is most effective in reducing the physical symptoms of stress, such as muscle tension. It is usually easiest to do sitting or lying down.

Begin by making yourself as comfortable as possible and by breathing nice and slowly (in fact, it's not a bad idea to begin with a short, abbreviated version of the controlled breathing method outlined on page 41).

Once your breathing has settled into a nice, steady rhythm, and when you're ready, gently tense the muscles in your face and head as you breathe in, hold for a few seconds, then relax the muscles as you breathe out. Repeat this 2–3 times.

Please note: when you tense your muscles as described, don't do it to the extent that you're in pain. As a general rule, you should feel that you've tightened your muscles to about 60–70 per cent of their capacity, but not more than that.

Do the same for the muscles in your neck and shoulders, and repeat 2–3 times. Continue this process in a slow and deliberate way throughout your whole body, working your way down from your head to your toes, and spending more time on those areas where you feel you experience more tension (common trouble spots, especially for those who spend too much time in front of a computer, are the jaw, shoulders and neck). Relax your muscles more and more as you progress through the exercise.

Don't forget, practise is the key. If you can practise this method at least once or twice each day, even if only for a few minutes, and even if you don't work through your whole body but just focus on your particular needs and trouble spots, you'll gradually master the skill of relaxation and, importantly, get better at noticing tension building much earlier. You'll then be in a better position to effectively ward off the accumulation of tension over time.

Take a rest; a field that has rested gives a bountiful crop.
Ovid, 43 BC–17 AD, Roman poet

27. Practise visual imagery relaxation

'Visual imagery relaxation' is very effective in creating feelings of calmness and tranquillity, and is the form of relaxation that most closely resembles meditation. It can be practised anywhere, but is typically easiest to do in a quiet, peaceful location.

Start by following the instructions below, but please note that the central premise here is to visualise anything you believe to be relaxing or calming, or even anything that's inspiring or motivating. Accordingly, feel free to experiment and come up with your own new ideas.

It's usually best to begin by making yourself as comfortable as you can and by slowing your breathing down until you've achieved a nice, steady rhythm. Take a few deep breaths, exhaling slowly and thinking calming, relaxing thoughts.

When you're ready, picture yourself in a beautiful location, where everything is as you would ideally have it. You may be on the beach, in a rainforest, by a lake or just at home in a nice comfortable chair. Imagine yourself as calm and relaxed as you could possibly be. You can feel your body is calm and relaxed. All you can hear is calming and relaxing. The sky is blue, the water is clear, and the chair is soft, warm and tantalisingly comfortable.

Play around with this concept and try a few different scenes until you find one you're really happy with. Involve all of your senses and assure yourself that you can return to this place whenever you want or need to relax.

I've said this before and I'll say it again – don't forget that practise is the key. Practise as often as you can, even if only for a few minutes (although I should note that with this technique, more so than with the others, you should probably set aside 10 minutes or more so you can fully immerse yourself in the scene) and, just as with the other strategies, you'll gradually master the skill and begin to realise the wonderful benefits of relaxation.

28. Sort out your sleep routine

On pages 29–30, I highlight the importance of making sure a good night's sleep becomes a habit. Here I want to talk about sleep hygiene, which refers to the basic 'dos' and 'don'ts' of good sleeping.

Below are some vital tips to follow that will help you improve your quality of sleep. Combined with the other sleep strategies outlined in this section, these tips will help you sort out your sleep routine.

- Avoid all stimulants at least 4–5 hours before going to sleep. This includes caffeine (eg coffee, tea and many soft drinks) as well as nicotine.
- Do not drink too much alcohol. Although alcohol might help you fall off to sleep it will also disturb your sleep. It can, for example, contribute to night-time waking and make it more likely that you will have to get up to empty your bladder during the night.
- Avoid heavy meals late at night. If you are hungry, have a simple, light snack.
- By all means exercise throughout the day, but do not exercise within 3–4 hours of wanting to go to sleep.
- Ensure your environment and physical situation is conducive to sleep. For example, make sure your room is dark and quiet, and your bed is comfortable.
- Avoid clock watching – this will only increase the chances of you feeling anxious and frustrated and will not help you sleep.
- Develop a pre-sleep routine. Begin a 'wind-down' about 1 hour before you want to go to sleep. Make this hour relaxing and, as much as possible, follow the same routine each night. Appropriate

activities might include having a warm bath or a cup of herbal tea, practising relaxation techniques or reading or listening to some quiet music.

A ruffled mind makes a restless pillow.
Charlotte Brontë, 1816–1855, English novelist

29. Keep your bedroom distraction-free

Even if you are putting effort into getting enough rest, the quality of your sleep can vary depending on how well you control your sleep environment. What you do, as well as when and where you do it, can affect how refreshed you feel in the morning.

The following guidelines show how you can adjust your sleep environment to optimise rest periods.

1. Go to bed only when you are tired and sleepy. Don't go to bed any earlier than is appropriate.
2. Do not use your bed for anything apart from sleep and sexual activity. Avoid eating, reading or watching television in bed. Even having a conversation with your partner (especially about anything that is emotional or stressful) is best done in some other place.
3. Don't stay in bed if you are having trouble getting to sleep. If you find yourself unable to fall asleep within about 20 minutes of going to bed, get up and do something relaxing or mundane for a few minutes, like reading a few pages of your book. Return to bed when you feel tired and sleepy.
4. Repeat Step 3 as often as you need to. Although this might be difficult in the short term, remind yourself of the long-term benefits of overcoming your sleep problem.
5. Get up at the same time every morning, even if you feel you have not slept well. Do not sleep in.
6. Do not sleep or nap through the day – this will only hamper your efforts to sleep at night.

Please note: Although the same basic principles will apply, exceptions should be made in certain circumstances, such as for parents with newborns, shift workers or people with certain health problems.

30. Switch off

Some of us live life at a faster pace, or experience greater amounts of stress on a regular basis. It is even more important for those of you who have a high-octane lifestyle to counteract this with appropriate periods of rest.

When faced with a challenge, humans react with what we call the stress response. This is what you will know as 'fight or flight'. Your heart rate goes up, your blood pressure rises, and your body releases hormones to mobilise you. When this response is constantly activated, however, the body is subject to elevated blood-sugar levels, lowered immunity, poor mental function and hypertension, amongst other things. At high stress levels, the body is simply unable to recover.

Professional athletes provide an interesting case study for balancing highly stressful activity with rest. One such research study investigated the habits of top-ranking tennis players.

Wanting to understand what, if anything, separated the top few players from the rest, the investigators measured and analysed a range of variables in an effort to see what it was that higher performing athletes did differently.

Among other things, they found that the top players had a much lower resting pulse rate in between points than their peers who performed at a lower level.

What does this mean? Well, it could mean many things, but my interpretation is that these top players were much better at 'switching off' when they didn't need to be 'on'. If you think about it carefully, there's no need to be 'on' all the time, and in fact if a player is 'switched on' or hyped up all the time then much energy will be wasted.

There's no doubt that elite athletes are highly focussed when they need to be, but they also seem to be very good at conserving energy during periods of rest.

Whether you're an elite athlete or not, there's an important message in this for all of us: there are many times when we could and should 'switch off', and that by doing so we'd be appropriately and effectively saving valuable energy.

So when could you take a rest and save your energy? Are there times when you could 'switch off' and allow your body and mind to recover and regenerate? Monitor the more stressful periods in your life and make sure to counter these with periods of rest, using relaxation techniques, for example, if they have proven helpful to you.

31. Put down your burden

A lecturer, when explaining stress management to a class, raised a glass of water and asked, 'How heavy is this glass of water?' The answers called out ranged from 20 grams to 500 grams.

Then the lecturer replied, 'The absolute weight doesn't matter. It depends on how long you try to hold it.'

'If I hold it for a minute, that's not a problem. If I hold it for an hour, I'll have an ache in my right arm. If I hold it for a day, you'll have to call an ambulance. In each case, it's the same weight, but the longer I hold it, the heavier it becomes.'

He continued, 'And that's the way it is with stress management. If we carry our burdens all the time, sooner or later, as the burden becomes increasingly heavy, we won't be able to carry on. As with the glass of water, you have to put it down for a while and rest before holding it again. When we're refreshed, we can carry on with the burden.'

This lesson is particularly salient for those who have jobs which require them to be on call around the clock. The advent of mobile phones, personal organisers and email have meant we are rarely able to leave work behind.

Before you return home tonight, put down the burden of work. Don't carry it with you – you can pick it up again tomorrow. Whatever other burdens you're carrying, put them down for a moment too if you can. Relax, then pick them up later after you've rested. Life is too short!

32. Keep an exercise log

To maximise the productivity of your exercise and relaxation sessions, to motivate yourself to continue and to better understand your body, start a diary of all the exercise and relaxation practice you do and how you feel during and after each activity.

For example, next to every diary entry or event, record the time spent exercising, the activity, and how intense the session was – easy, medium or hard. A good yardstick for measuring your fitness level is recording your pulse rate on waking each morning (as you get fitter, you should find that your resting pulse rate gradually decreases). Alternatively, think about how calm you feel before and after a relaxation session, and record this daily. If you're feeling ambitious, you can add another layer of complexity to the exercise by rating how you felt after each session in terms of happiness and satisfaction.

Reflect on your diary: which events energised you or filled you with joy, excitement or happiness (or any other positive emotion, for that matter)? What events drained you or led to misery, stress, anxiety or depression (or any other negative emotion, for that matter)?

Keeping a log of your exercise progress not only gives you a positive record of all that you have done, but holds you accountable for the effort you are putting in. It gives you an opportunity to raise the bar as you increase your fitness, and challenge yourself anew. Reward the time that you put into your body, and be proud of your accomplishments, no matter how small.

33. Snack on something healthy

Next time you feel like a snack (or preferably *before* you actually feel like a snack, because by that time you've already allowed yourself to get hungrier than you probably should) choose a fresh, healthy one rather than opting for foods high in fat and sugar. Instead of bombarding your body with empty nutrition, think of eating as investing in your wellbeing – good fuel will mean your body runs better.

There's no doubt that choosing healthy snacks will not only make you feel better in the short term, but you'll also be doing your body a favour in the long term. So stock up on the following healthy foods and enjoy them in moderation:

- fresh fruit
- fresh vegetables
- small amounts of dried fruit
- low-fat yoghurt
- low-fat, high-fibre muffins
- unsalted nuts and grains.

This is a habit which will become second nature, and the benefits will grow from these small dietary modifications. You will likely find that you crave healthier foods when hungry, rather than quick-fix snacks.

34. Re-hydrate yourself

Happiness requires energy and dehydration leads to lethargy. So it stands to reason that happiness, at least in part, requires adequate hydration – quite simply, this comes from drinking enough water every day.

Water is far more effective for quenching thirst than carbonated soft drinks and fruit juices. As simple as it sounds, water is really good for you, and for most of us, achieving an adequate intake requires increasing our current consumption and being consciously aware of drinking regularly.

Although there's some debate about the amount of water we need to drink daily, health bodies tend to recommend drinking somewhere between 8 and 14 cups each day. Variables that determine the exact amount required include the amount of exercise you do, the climate in which you live and your age and health status (so if you have any health concerns it's probably worthwhile consulting your doctor or a good nutritionist about the best approach for you).

Nevertheless, we should all aim to drink a minimum of 8 cups each day and that, in simple terms, is about one cup for every hour and a half we're awake.

The good news is that most of us in the 'developed world' have access to drinkable tap water, which doesn't cost anything, so keep a glass on your desk or have a drink bottle close at hand all the time. Make drinking water a habit. Use regular drink breaks to 'switch off' or to refresh and renew for a few seconds every hour.

35. Make activity vigorous

If you're currently unfit you'll probably find that any attempts you make to exercise will lead to tiredness (and maybe even soreness and pain). However, this should be seen as nothing more than just a short-term side effect, as the longer-term benefits of exercising include, without any doubt whatsoever, increased energy levels and improved mood.

As already mentioned, exercise is one of the most effective and powerful methods for fighting depression and enhancing happiness, not to mention one of the quickest, easiest and arguably the cheapest. But for exercise to work it needs to be practised regularly. There is no consensus on how much exercise is necessary to maintain health, and the exact amount each of us requires will vary, depending on factors such as age, health and individual goals.

In simple terms, however, most would agree that as well as engaging in as much activity as we can every day, we should also actively engage in vigorous exercise (that's when you get hot, sweaty and out of breath) for at least 30–40 minutes, at least 4–5 times each week.

Create an exercise plan for yourself, plotting regular exercise along with a gradual increase in the time spent exerting yourself and the intensity of the exercise. You can find free fitness plans on the internet, in books in your local library, or you can ask a friend with some experience in programs to help you construct a personal plan. These need not be complicated, you can simply aim to take a brisk walk for half an hour every Monday, Wednesday and Friday, for example.

Once you have committed to an activity on paper there will be far more motivation to complete it, as with any other goal-driven activity. Exercise regimes are not just for athletes! So find a way to engage in some fun exercise most, if not every, day.

36. Increase incidental activity

Incidental activity involves finding ways to keep active in your normal, daily life; it shouldn't require any additional effort or expenditure of time, as it simply involves modifying what you're already doing to live a more active life. It's probably best explained by giving a few simple examples. You could:

- Walk up the stairs whenever you can rather than hopping in a lift or on an escalator.
- Walk to the local shops rather than driving.
- Get off your bus or train a stop early and walk part of the way to work or school.
- Instead of eating lunch at your desk, find a sunny spot outside.
- Park farther away from your destination.
- Carry your groceries home.
- Walk down the corridor to talk to someone at work rather than sending them an email or talking to them on the phone.

Practising incidental activity can significantly improve your health and wellbeing without requiring you to set aside time specifically to exercise, and without you ever needing to set foot in a gym or health club.

37. Accept your body

The reality is that 'beautiful' people are not necessarily any happier than the rest of us. Despite what many people think, being more attractive will not increase our happiness. So, unless you're significantly over- or underweight, or unless your body is 'unhealthy', accept your body, your face, your hair colour and all the other things that are 'you', for what they are.

Because for some of us this might be easier said than done, you might find it helpful to consider the following points:

- Once you are past your mid-twenties you will not grow in height.
- You can 'change' the colour of your hair and even the colour of your eyes, but you will always know who and what you really are.
- If you're significantly over- or underweight, you should certainly consider consulting a doctor, nutritionist, dietician, exercise physiologist or clinical psychologist and find out how to achieve a healthier weight range, but there's actually very little you can do to change the shape of your body (excluding surgery, which carries with it considerable risks and consequences).

Studies have shown that each person has an inbuilt weight range which they naturally return to. Similarly, you have an inbuilt happiness range within which you move, regardless of your body shape. The level of your happiness is much easier to alter than your physique, so start by identifying what it is that you like about your body.

Avoid thinking about your body as merely an object, but as a vessel or machine that allows you to be active, to perform tasks and to be affectionate toward those you love. Athletic bodies are not always skinny – swimmers require a level of body fat to improve their buoyancy, and downhill skiers require bulky quadriceps, hamstrings and gluteal muscles to counteract the forces operating on them as they descend at high speeds. The point is that each athlete maximises their existing strengths and engages in a sport that exploits their natural physicality. If you appreciate your body for its abilities, you will feel far more positive about it.

> *Happiness can exist only in acceptance.*
> George Orwell, 1903–1950, English novelist

38. Listen to your body

Part of training your body and pushing it to its limits is giving it time to recover. Understanding how your body responds to work is as important as getting to know your personality, and will have an impact on how productive your efforts are.

Consider any weaknesses when engaging in physical activity – choose sports that don't exacerbate existing injuries, and be sure to treat trouble spots carefully. By regarding your body as an athlete would regard theirs, you will gain a greater respect for yourself, and feel more inclined to consider what you put into your body as well as how you think about it.

When you are engaging in cardiovascular activity, try pushing yourself harder for 10–15 seconds, then see how long it takes you to recover. Exploring the limits and potential of your own body will help you to tailor exercise toward your strengths. Also, the more in tune you are with your body, the less likely it is that you will suffer injury.

39. Stretch

Though we understand that our minds need time to rest, and are familiar with the idea of relaxation, we often identify exercise as exertion; resulting in a rapid heart rate and sweat. But an equally important part of exercise is the warm up and cool down – and one of the key elements here is stretching. Preparing your body for work is no different to preparing yourself to confront a difficult situation. Stretching helps to activate your muscles and protect yourself from injury.

Stretching is also intrinsically beneficial. Gentle exercise can be relaxing and allow you to get in touch with your body. You wouldn't conduct a seminar at work without a debrief, would you? Think of taking the time to release and loosen your muscles at the end of a workout or busy day as the same process.

40. Laugh!

Laughter has been clinically shown to relax the body, improve mental functioning, boost your immunity, connect you to others and, of course, bolster your mood. Think of laughter as preventative medicine – a vitamin of sorts, which you need to take regularly.

Finding out what makes you laugh is similar to, and perhaps easier than, finding out what your goals and values are. Aim to include activities in your day-to-day life that make you laugh, and try to see the funny side of things. You could also consider inducing voluntary laughter. If you have ever tried not to laugh, you will have probably found it impossible – similarly, once you begin to laugh voluntarily you will find that natural laughter follows. For the adventurous among you, commit to joining a laughter club – yes, they do exist!

> *The most wasted of all days is one without laughter.*
> E.E. Cummings, 1894–1962, American poet

Section Three

20 ways to better relationships

We know from research, and you will know anecdotally, that the happiest people tend to have lots of friends, build supportive relationships and often spend time with other happy people. Building lasting and loving relationships is not solely about the other person, but begins with yourself. Understanding your own needs and styles of communication are as important as learning to convey your affection and emotions, as well as building trust. Great friendships do not just happen, but require investment and maintenance. One of the most unlimited sources of happiness, relationships are the cornerstones of who we are and how we live our lives.

41. Cut comparisons

Forget about the Joneses. When it comes to happiness, comparisons are rarely, if ever, helpful. Happiness is a subjective phenomenon; it is experienced differently by everyone and it means different things to different people. As the saying goes, one man's meat is another man's poison – our needs and desires vary, so what makes one person happy might not have the same impact on the next person.

Although most of us realise the disparity between our individual requirements, it is easy to fall into the trap of looking over the fence, seeing what the neighbours have and thinking that we need that too. Quite simply, this is unhelpful and almost certainly a direct path to unhappiness.

Research strongly indicates that those who are happiest appreciate what they have and focus less on what they don't have. Long-term happiness studies have shown that wealth, geographical location, climate and race have little to no effect on a person's level of happiness. The same body of research clearly purports that, rather than judging themselves in relation to others, happy people simply clarify what's important to them and then focus on achieving and fulfilling their priorities.

So with this in mind, to achieve happiness you need to work out what it means for you, and determine what you need to do to build more of this into your life. Don't compare yourself to others – happiness comes tailor-made!

42. Practise affirmation

There's a risk that what's about to come might sound corny or clichéd, but I'll still write it because I think it's vitally important: I honestly believe that each and every one of you reading this, each and every person you know, and in fact each and every person in the world, has the potential to be absolutely fantastic, a world champion . . . at something.

Without being modest, write down what it is that you most value about yourself. Write down the achievements you are most proud of and what you like best about your body. Meditate and focus on this. (These notes can help you work out what you can do to make the most of these attributes and qualities.)

Equally important is the need to value others. Your family and friends are often the people that you look up to most, and yet we rarely stop to consider how they reflect on us, on who we are as people. Take the time to think about the 'greatness' in your family and friends.

Write a list of the people who are most important to you, and next to each name note down what it is you most value about this person and your relationship with them.

Remember how great you feel when you receive the respect and affection of family and friends, and take opportunities to offer affirmation of them in return. Relationships should be ever-strengthening; the more effort and heart you put in, the more you will find you gain.

The world is not perfect, and I'm well aware of the many troubles and problems, injustices and evils that abound, but I'm also aware there are many heroes, life-savers, inventors, entrepreneurs and kind and loving people doing wonderful and generous acts.

So next time you think about how bad the world is, stop for a minute or two and think about all the great things that happen every day, and all the great people there are doing amazing deeds.

There is much to celebrate in yourself, your family, your friends and the world around you. Take the time to reflect regularly and you will reinforce the affirmation.

Write it on your heart that every day is the best day in the year.

Ralph Waldo Emerson, 1803–1882, American essayist and poet

43. Spend time with positive people

I'd like to provide a caveat to this suggestion before I even start. I'm not in any way suggesting that we abandon those in need or ignore family or friends who're distressed and could benefit from our support, love or help (especially during difficult times).

That said, happy people spend more time with other happy people. Happiness and positivity are contagious, so the more time you spend in the company of positive people the more you'll bask in their happy and healthy energy.

Conversely, sometimes family members or friends can have a negative effect on our mood. A judgemental friend may not focus on your strengths, and a pessimistic one will be unlikely to foster your self-esteem. If someone seems to be 'pulling you down' you simply need to spend less time with them. It can be hard enough to remain positive without someone else emphasising the negative! If you do not receive the respect that you know you deserve, then do not give that person's opinions any validity.

If there is someone you know who always seems sunny and engaging, make a conscious effort to spend more time with them. Suggest an activity that you can both enjoy, and let them know how pleasant they are to be around. Spend your lunch hour with a colleague who likes to take a walk around the city, instead of spending it with a colleague who likes to read quietly. If you meet other parents at your child's school who seem effervescent, suggest you have a joint picnic outing. There is no reason to stop making friends as you grow older and settle into a routine, so get out there!

44. Be supportive

As I have mentioned, there's absolutely no doubt that happy people have both more and better quality relationships. Consider the following story:

> A guy was walking down the street when he fell into a giant pothole. It was so deep he couldn't get out, so he started to yell.
>
> A jazz musician passed by and heard the man calling, 'Help! I fell in a hole!'
>
> The musician looked in and nodded. He got out his saxophone and played a soulful, bluesy ballad and then walked on.
>
> Soon a priest walked by and heard the man yelling, 'Father! I fell in this hole, can you help me out?'
>
> The priest obligingly pencilled a prayer, bowed his head, threw it down the hole and strolled on in silence.
>
> Then a friend walked by and heard the man screaming.
>
> 'Hey Bill! It's me, Sam! I fell in here, can you help me out?'
>
> So Bill jumped in the hole. Sam said, 'Are you crazy? Now we're both stuck down here!'
>
> Bill answered, 'Yes, but I've been down here before and I know the way out.'

I believe that good quality positive relationships are based on inter-dependence between the two parties. While self-reliance is an admirable trait, it can alienate you, whereas using each other for support actually reinforces your bond.

We have all heard of fair-weather friends who are not around when the going gets tough. Alternatively, if you can be supportive when it counts, your value as a friend will skyrocket. Next time you hear of a friend in need, think about how best you can help. Work out how much time you can spare, and match your skills with their needs.

This might involve:

- cooking a meal for them
- looking after their kids for an afternoon
- suggesting an outing that will give them a break from their troubles
- sending flowers or some small token to let them know they are in your thoughts.

45. Focus on people's strengths

The best relationships are frequently built on recognition of each other's strengths. Individuals within strong relationships realise no one is perfect, but at the same time recognise that each and every person has unique qualities and attributes which, when appreciated, allow for love, compassion and respect to grow and blossom.

Too often, problems within relationships stem from one or both parties focussing too much on the other person's faults, weaknesses and limitations. This, not surprisingly, leads to frustration, irritation and, at worst, bitterness and hatred.

To boost the quality of your relationships and to experience more happiness as a result, find some time to sit down and think about those people who are most important in your life and then list, consider and meditate upon their strengths. What is it, for example, that makes them wonderful? What is it, for example, that they bring to the relationship that no one else could? What is it that makes them special, good and likeable to you?

46. Be an unconditional friend

It has been my experience that people who have more good quality relationships tend to think the best of others more often.

Until you have evidence to the contrary, I recommend you try to assume the best in others. In Australia we've always had a 'fair go' philosophy; it's far better to occasionally be proved wrong, and possibly to have someone take advantage of you or mistreat you, than to spend your life experiencing the unpleasant emotions that accompany constant mistrust of others.

When a suspicious or negative thought toward a friend springs up in your mind, challenge it, and construct an opposing thought. Give that person the benefit of the doubt. Start off all your interactions with a degree of unconditional positive regard and embed this in all your relationships. By doing so, you'll experience much more positivity in the connections you make.

47. Be purposeful in your relationships

This might sound obvious, but sometimes we take the simple things in life for granted. Largely it's how we go about the simple things that tends to differentiate those who are happy and successful from those who aren't.

Every interaction within each relationship has a purpose – and the purpose will vary each time. Consider, for example, the purpose of a meeting at work versus the purpose of a discussion with a friend while catching up for coffee.

The purpose of meeting a friend for coffee might simply be to update each other regarding your personal and social lives, while the purpose of the work-related example might be to achieve a specific outcome that will move you closer to your stated goals. Because the purpose in each scenario is quite different, the way you should approach each interaction should also be quite different. Tailor your behaviour to the relationship that you are tending.

Next time you're about to enter into a conversation or interact with someone in any context, ask yourself, 'What's the purpose of this conversation and how can I best achieve what I want to here?' If you want to have an intimate, affectionate relationship with your partner, you need to emphasise these traits the next time you sit down to eat with them – be affectionate, open and honest. Your behaviour here would vary greatly from that at a business lunch, where you would probably want to speak succinctly and demonstrate through your body language that you are confident and well-prepared.

48. Accentuate the positive

Both my coaching experience and my reading of the relevant research have taught me that positive relationships are, not surprisingly, filled with more positive interactions. To boost the positivity in your relationships, try to shine the light on what's right. Too many people focus only on problems and mistakes, and only raise an issue with another person when something is wrong (all too often ignoring things when all is going well). This is the exact opposite of what we know works, so flip it around and realise the benefits of having happy relationships.

Unless you really need to react, ignore minor irritations and instead try to highlight positives and successes when you notice them in others. Actively look for other people doing good things – catch them when they're doing something right, not just when they're doing something wrong.

Try this with at least one person over the next week (your partner, your child, or a colleague at work). Actively congratulate and praise this other person when they do something you consider desirable, worthwhile or good.

49. Outweigh the negatives with positives

Marcial Losada is a famous mathematician and psychologist who achieved a degree of fame as the result of a body of work he produced investigating relationships.

In short, what has come to be known as the 'Losada Ratio' is the proportion of positive to negative comments made within a particular interaction. Losada devised the minimum ratio of good to bad comments to establish a good relationship, depending on the type of interaction.

The ratio is 5:1 in intimate personal relationships (such as those between a husband and wife) and 3:1 in workplace relationships. That is, for every negative or critical comment you make to someone, you should make at least 5 positive, supportive and encouraging comments (or 3 if at work), if you want that relationship to flourish and to enhance your happiness and the happiness of the other person.

We now know that those who fall below a certain point (the ratio) are significantly less likely to flourish and have positive relationships. It's a fairly easy thing to measure, and you may be surprised at just how much better your interactions become by applying this simple but well-tested formula.

50. Communicate effectively

We can all recognise the difference between simply talking and communicating. Communicating implies that both parties involved are engaged and have the same understanding of what is being discussed – it will lead to more productive outcomes, and will most likely ease tensions where there is conflict. It is worthwhile giving your communication skills a brush-up – here are a few pointers to get you started.

Begin by evaluating what it is that goes through your mind before, during and after a conversation or interaction.

Conversations are not one-way affairs, and so it is crucial that you acknowledge the other person's opinion and perspective. Accept they have a right to believe what they believe. Once you have understood the other person, you can assert your own position, beliefs and needs.

Listen carefully to what the other person has to say. An open communicator reacts and responds to the other person's dialogue, and adjusts their own comments accordingly. Avoid cutting the other person off, and take turns to make your points.

It is obviously okay to experience emotions during any interaction, but in the majority of cases you'll understand and communicate more effectively if you try to keep as calm as possible. Enunciate your own opinions in a relaxed tone; try to keep a check on the volume and pitch of your voice: the more excitable you become, the less likely the other person will be to listen to what you are saying.

51. Be affirmative in conversation

Your efforts to communicate will be far more likely to succeed if you can understand how assertive communication differs from communication that might be referred to as aggressive or passive.

Passive communication is when you don't express yourself the way you would like to. Typical reasons for this include: wanting to please (or not wanting to upset) others; being afraid of confrontation; or not being confident about your ability to manage confrontation.

Although in the short term you might avoid unpleasant situations, conflicts and tension, in the longer term this type of communication frequently leads to feelings of frustration, anxiety, disappointment and anger. Furthermore, this approach often means that you are not expressing yourself adequately, and are certainly not achieving what you want to achieve.

Aggressive communication is when you express yourself or your needs at the expense of others', without consideration for other people's feelings. Typical reasons for this include wanting to dominate or humiliate other people or not wanting to be dominated or controlled by others.

Although in the short term you might get what you want – you may feel 'superior' and as though you have vented your anger – in the longer term this approach is often associated with feelings of embarrassment and guilt. Other people will also often feel hurt and vengeful.

Assertive communication is, quite simply, the ideal. Assertiveness occurs when you express yourself and your needs in an appropriate, direct and thoughtful way, taking into account the feelings and needs of others.

The intention behind this approach is to communicate fairly and effectively. The aim is to get what you want, while also trying to ensure that as often as possible, others also get what they want.

This approach has both immediate and long-term advantages. You are more likely to feel good about yourself and others are more likely to respect and admire you. Notably, you are more likely to achieve your objective, often without the other person being harmed in the process. At the end of the day both parties are more likely to feel good about what has happened and the relationship will be strengthened.

The next time you face a conflict situation, assess what the other person's thoughts, needs and feelings are, before putting forward your own opinions. Think these through before you announce them, and word them in a neutral way. You can actually develop your social intuition through successfully navigating these kinds of situations.

52. Choose your words

An important component of effective communication is the ability to assess each situation on its merits. Although we can generally say that assertive communication is better than either passive or aggressive communication, there are not really any 'right' or 'wrong' ways of communicating – instead, different situations require different approaches. Taking this into account, there are certain strategies that, along with those already described, will help you to communicate effectively in more situations.

Remember that not everyone always agrees about the way things should be done. So rather than saying 'This is how it should be ...' it is usually best to express your needs by using statements such as 'I want ...' or 'I would like ...'. If this is followed by a description of a specific behaviour, then the person receiving the message should be clear about what your needs are.

Similarly, it is useful to include statements that accurately describe how you feel. While doing so, it is important not to blame the other person by saying things like 'You make me feel ...'. Rather, it is less confrontational, and more helpful to say something like 'When you did X, I felt ...'.

Choose the moment carefully: timing is of the essence, particularly if you are discussing an issue that is complex or potentially distressing. Ideally, try to find a time when you will not feel rushed, be too tired or when distractions and interruptions will interfere with your discussion.

Practise. Run through in your mind what you would like to say and how you would like to say it. Even better, say it out loud. And better still, practise in front of a friend or relative and ask them for feedback. Don't forget, practise makes for proficiency.

53. Foster your intimate relationship

Research tells us that happiness depends to some extent on having a good quality relationship, yet divorce rates are rising and the average number and duration of marriages is falling.

A satisfying and fulfilling relationship is sought after by the vast majority of people, so why is this so difficult to achieve?

Although it's important to spend quality time on relationships, there's no substitute for quantity! So make sure you call, email, text or, best of all, meet up with your loved one on a regular basis. Do this as often as you can and I guarantee the return on your investment will be enormous in the currency of happiness.

Whether you believe that your current relationship is particularly unfulfilling or generally pretty good, you can always improve its quality by making small changes.

The following list of suggestions incorporates skills and concepts that have been taken from research into flourishing relationships. While they are written with intimate relationships in mind, many of the strategies can be applied to friendships and family relationships as well.

- Long-term, mutually fulfilling relationships rarely happen easily or without effort. Many of our beliefs about relationships and romance are simply unrealistic, and we can blame Hollywood for much of this! Fulfilling relationships have little to do with luck and more to do with a willingness to make the relationship a priority and to put in a focussed effort.
- A relationship starts with you, so make sure you are satisfied with who you are as an individual, and with other aspects of your life.

A relationship is more likely to be successful if it consists of two complete individuals, rather than if one partner is relying on the relationship to make them 'whole'.

- Communicate. Even if you've been in a relationship for a long time and you know the other person very well, no one can read minds. Try to avoid that common pitfall of assuming your partner knows what you are thinking.

- Be respectful and constructive in your disagreements. This is often a hard one, but research shows that couples who can see their partner's perspective during arguments have considerably fewer and shorter disagreements. Ensure you agree on what you are actually arguing about, and understand that it is not the two of you against each other; it is both of you against the problem.

- Compromise. While it is important to be assertive in a relationship and make your needs clear, it is also essential that both partners compromise in some areas. You are two individuals with different histories and personalities, and should expect differences in opinions and preferences. Try to respect those differences, and even appreciate them!

- Be unselfish. Unfortunately it can be easy to focus exclusively on how a relationship is making you fulfilled and happy, and what you think your partner should be doing to facilitate this. But the happiest of relationships involve both partners striving to ensure the happiness and wellbeing of the other one. Make it routine to go out of your way to do something for your partner's sake that won't necessarily directly benefit you.

- Openly show your love and appreciation. Happy couples tend to show their happiness with each other more openly than dissatisfied couples. Don't assume your partner knows you love and appreciate them just because you may have been together a long time. Tell them as often as you can, particularly in relation to specific things (eg 'I really appreciate it that you always do the washing-up without me having to ask').

- Don't be afraid to say, 'I'm sorry' and 'Thank you'. These two simple phrases can significantly reduce arguments and shorten the length of post-argument 'hangovers'. Even if you think that your partner 'should' do a certain chore, saying thank you is still appreciated and provides reinforcement so your partner is more likely to do it again (and feel happy about it).

- Don't compare your relationship with other relationships: this is rarely helpful. Each relationship is different, and other relationships can often seem more ideal than they really are, which just leaves you feeling dissatisfied with your own situation.

- Be patient and understanding with your partner. No one is perfect, but this can be easy to forget sometimes!

- Find a happy medium by spending some time together and some time on your own. Of course, quality time together as a couple is important in maintaining a satisfying relationship, but most people also require time to themselves. Find activities that you enjoy doing together, but don't necessarily force your preferences on your partner when it may be much more enjoyable for you to engage in some activities alone or with another friend.

- Don't wait to start making the changes that you feel will improve the quality of your relationship; start making them now! How often do you put things off until later when you think you will have more time, energy or motivation? If you know the direction in which you want to head, start today and make small changes and small efforts each day. This will help you achieve the fulfilling relationship that you are seeking.

> *Love at first sight is easy to understand; it's when two people have been looking at each other for a lifetime that it becomes a miracle.*
>
> Amy Bloom, born 1953, American writer

54. Be a do-gooder

Many of the previous tips for building positive relationships have, in one way or another, encouraged you to think about doing good things to and for others. In most cases, we think about doing good things for others when there's a specific reason – maybe they've done something nice for us or we simply want to show them we love them.

That's all well and good, but I also encourage you to think about practising random acts of kindness; that is, doing good, caring, loving and positive things for others for no reason at all. Research has shown that altruism is a powerful catalyst for happiness, perhaps because it gratifies often overlooked values and drives in the human psyche.

We can all help bring happiness to our friends, neighbours and communities – even the smallest gesture can make a difference in someone's life. Try some of the following and see how good it makes you feel:

- Offer a few hours of free babysitting to a stressed-out single parent in your neighbourhood.
- When you buy food from a vending machine, slip in some extra money. The next person to use the machine will be grateful for the free snack.
- Mow the lawn or cook a meal for an elderly neighbour.
- Next time you eat out at a restaurant, leave a thank-you note along with your tip.
- Pay someone a compliment.
- Donate new children's books to a local school or library.
- Visit a local nursing home and spend a few minutes chatting with the residents. Even better, take flowers to brighten up their rooms.

- Buy a grocery bag full of nutritious canned goods and donate it to your local charity.
- Track down your favourite teachers and send them letters telling them what an inspiration they've been to you over the years.

55. Pay a celebration visit

Positive psychology has pioneered an exercise that has proven time and time again to give an immediate boost in happiness levels to everyone involved. The 'celebration visit' is essentially an affirmation – an opportunity to let other people know that you appreciate and love them, are grateful for what they've done, and that you want to celebrate this with them in a tangible way. Put into practice, it can have a profound impact on your relationships.

As with many of the strategies and tips proposed by positive psychologists, there are various ways of performing such a gesture. Consider one or all of the following options when planning your celebration visit:

- List all of the people in your life to whom you feel genuine gratitude (your parents, partner, children, other family members, friends, past teachers or mentors).
- Call them and tell them honestly and sincerely how you feel.
- Write them a letter expressing your love and gratitude.
- Give them a copy of your thoughts and feelings on paper – frame it or preserve it in some way for them to keep.
- Visit this person and read them your letter, or tell them face-to-face how much they mean to you and how grateful you are for what they've done.

One variation on this theme is the celebration night, where a group of people get together, each having brought someone they want to celebrate, and affirm this person in public.

Remember, big acts can have big effects, so don't be afraid to open up. Occasions for reflection such as this are all too rare, and we do not, as a culture, make a habit of reinforcing our bonds.

Kind words do not cost much. Yet they accomplish much.
Blaise Pascal, 1623–1662, French mathematician, physicist and theologian

56. Give generously

Happiness is surely one of the most sought-after goals in the world, yet it is also one of the most elusive. Why, when we know so much about the key variables that contribute to our happiness, do so many people miss the mark?

Quite simply, because they look in the wrong places! Instead of focussing inwards, happy people spend more time focussing outwards. Whilst they care for themselves, live healthy lives, and attend to the challenge of negative thoughts as well as the reinforcement of positive ones, they also actively engage in activities that will benefit others. Rather than being selfish and self-centred, they are more generous and altruistic.

The inspirational Helen Keller was once quoted as saying, 'Many persons have a wrong idea of what constitutes true happiness. It is not attained through self-gratification but through fidelity to a worthy purpose.' Having a clear sense of purpose in life is, interestingly, one of the core strategies that will increase your chances of happiness. If this purpose involves the benefit of others, then you increase your likelihood of experiencing real and meaningful positive emotions even further.

There is a wonderful law of nature that goes like this: 'The three things we crave most in life – happiness, freedom, and peace of mind – are always attained by giving them to someone else.' And there are many ways we can give to others, just as there are many ways we can become happy ourselves.

Donate money – you only need to give as much as you can afford to give. Donate time – there are innumerable organisations who'd love a helping hand. Give generously of your skills and experience. Simply taking the time to listen to someone can make a world of difference.

If happiness is something you'd like to experience more of, then clarify your life purpose and think optimistically, develop positive relationships with others and live healthily, but most of all don't forget that one of the most powerful sources of happiness is engagement in charitable acts. Give, and there's no doubt you'll receive!

57. Lean on others

Though no one wants to be a drain on their family or friends, interdependence is a key component of successful relationships. Trust is bound up in our ability to support our friends when they need it, as well as our willingness to be open with them and share our problems. As the saying goes, 'a problem shared is a problem halved'.

Often we underestimate how crucial human relationships are to our own wellbeing, yet studies have shown, time and time again, that trust is one of the best indicators of life satisfaction. Being able to trust your neighbours, colleagues and family is critical in forming positive relationships with them; trust is the lynchpin of a healthy society.

Ask your neighbours to look after your pet when you go away, and offer a reciprocal favour. Ask for your children's input in family affairs to make them feel a part of the process. The more interdependence you build into your life, the less 'work' you are effectively taking on alone.

> *No man is an island, entire of itself; every man is a piece*
> *of the continent, a part of the main.*
> John Donne, 1572–1631, English poet

58. Enlist a happiness buddy

Why are more and more people paying good money to personal trainers to help them exercise? It's not because they don't know what to do. Most people already know how to walk, run, do sit-ups and push-ups. Instead, the reason is that many of us need to have someone who'll hold us accountable.

Even if you know what to do, when it comes to boosting your happiness you will probably struggle sometimes to have the discipline that's necessary to stick to 'the program' every day. Much of what's in this book could be labelled commonsense, but having worked as a clinical and coaching psychologist for over fifteen years it's obvious to me that commonsense is not necessarily common practice.

To increase your chances of applying all the strategies that are important and relevant to you, consider finding yourself a 'happiness buddy'. This could be a professional such as a qualified coach or some other appropriately-trained health professional, or it could be a friend or colleague who shares your desire to be happier.

Once you've found the right person, discuss your plans and goals and then organise to meet on a regular basis to 'check in' with each other or to 'check up' on each other. Think of it in the same way you would a book club – if you commit to attending the club every month you're more likely to read the selected books. Similarly, if you commit to meet your friend every week or month to discuss happiness strategies, you'll increase your chances of successfully practising these very important life skills.

59. Have a friend affirm you

This exercise involves constructing a profile of the ways in which other people believe you make positive contributions. It involves contacting about 20 people who know you relatively well (and ideally people from different parts of your life who've seen you in different contexts, such as personal friends, relatives and work colleagues) and asking them to provide you with three examples of positive contributions you have made.

The simplest way to do this is to send them an email, or phone or visit them and ask them to think about their interactions with you, and to identify the times when you were at your best. In responding, ask them to provide specific examples so you can understand the situation and the characteristics they're describing.

You will not only receive a self-esteem boost and gain insight into your strengths, but you'll feel very positive toward the people who respond, and will be fostering a sense of interdependence in the relationship.

60. Reflect on criticism positively

We can sometimes find our strengths by looking to our weaknesses, or faults. Is there something in your life that other people have always told you to improve, increase, reduce or somehow change?

If so, have you ever tried to change this thing, and struggled? Have you ever found that you just can't be what they want you to be?

What might be going on here is that you're trying to change an innate, personal strength, which is an extremely difficult thing to do, and not such a great idea. A different approach, and one that I'd much more strongly recommend, is to take the comments others have made and find the essence of their thought. Then work out what's actually going on and whether, in fact, you can turn this 'problem' around and build on it in a positive way. Because if you can find a constructive outlet or channel for this 'fault', which in reality is probably an underutilised strength, then you'll almost certainly find that you'll experience more happiness and success in all areas of your life. For example:

- If you've ever been told you need to 'toughen up', maybe one of your strengths is empathy.
- If you've ever been told you need to 'keep focussed on one task', maybe one of your strengths is creativity.
- If you've ever been told you're 'too stubborn', maybe one of your strengths is perseverance.

Another way to identify your strengths is to consider whether there are things for which you've always or often been praised, or whether there are tasks that other people often ask you to do. Although in some situations this might be frustrating, it could also be taken as a compliment. Ask yourself, 'Why do people always ask me to organise things/ take minutes/ lead the project?' And the answer is probably because they see strengths in you that you might not even be aware of. Go back to the points on the previous page and look for themes or patterns in compliments or requests. Can you identify anything in this that might reflect your strengths? If so, can you imagine how you could use these strengths or enjoy these activities more?

Section Four

20 ways to a more positive mind

Our brains are amazingly complex organs – far more complex than any super-computers. Discovering the subtleties of how our brains function can be a subject to which psychologists devote their entire careers. However enigmatic the human mind may prove, simply by appreciating its complexity we can gain power over the millions of thoughts we have each day. Positive psychology allows us to take back some of the power our intellects have over our everyday lives by altering the way we arrive at conclusions. It is also a potent tool for maximising the happiness that we do experience. You do not need to be born an optimist to think like one, as you will see when you read on.

61. Aim to play above the line!

As a clinical psychologist I learned much about alleviating distress, and found it extremely satisfying to know that I was helping people overcome problems such as depression, anxiety, anger and stress. But I also came to realise that as good as this was, helping people to reduce the distress in their lives wasn't always enabling them to be happier.

There's a significant and meaningful difference between an absence of distress and happiness. Though we focus our efforts on eliminating the negatives in our lives, we rarely focus on increasing the positives. If you imagine a graph plotting our emotional wellbeing with a vertical line drawn from minus-ten to plus-ten, many people, psychologists included, only focus on moving from minus-ten to zero (or 'mediocre').

Being happy is about aiming to live your life 'above the line'. It is about living in the plus-ten zone. Too many people spend their time thinking their lives would be better if only they could fix all their problems. This isn't such a bad idea, but what we know from research is that if you really want to experience the meaningful forms of happiness, you also need to spend time thinking about what's already good in your life and building on what already works. There's a big difference, with the latter option having a far more positive focus.

So ask yourself, where does your focus fall on the graph? Are you spending more time below the line than above? Select something that is working well in your life and consciously put energy into improving it. This could be a relationship, a hobby, your work environment, or something small such as a meal you make for yourself. There is no reason that something 'good' can't become something 'fantastic' with a little bit of effort.

62. Clarify your values

Review the following list of values, and single out your top five. Feel free to add others you believe are important.

accomplishment	comradeship	interdependence
acknowledgment	control	intimacy
adaptability	creativity	joy
adventure	excellence	knowledge
artistry	excitement	love
authenticity	family	making decisions
beauty and aesthetics	freedom	meeting challenges
being admired	friendship	money
being alone	fun and enjoyment	order
being different	helping others	participation
being valued	honesty	peace
being with others	humour	personal development
belonging	independence	physical health
change and variation	influencing others	power and authority
collaboration	integrity	profit
communication	intellectual stimulation	recognition
community	interaction with others	respect

security	spirituality	time
self-determination	stability	tranquillity
self-expression	status	zest
sensuality	success	
solitude	support	

What you will have now is a cheat sheet of your own core values. Recognising these values and trying to live your life according to them will lead to greater satisfaction, gratification, and, ultimately, happiness. If your core values are stability and family, understand that spending Saturday night at the karaoke bar is less likely to satiate these needs than, say, attending the local trivia night. Consider how you can change certain elements of your life to make them more consistent with your internal desires, and you will undoubtedly increase your chances of living with more happiness.

63. Repel antagonistic values

Every day we're bombarded by thousands of advertising and marketing messages that subtly (or in many cases not so subtly) tell us we'd be happier if we were thinner, wore certain clothes, drove the right car, drank specific soft drinks and so on. You probably realise that many of these messages are not entirely true or valid. Nevertheless, they tend to find their way into our minds (even if only on a subconscious level).

But you don't have to let them. Psychologists have long used 'on-task training' to help a range of people – from those with attention deficit disorder to corporate executives – wanting to maximise their efficiency and productivity. The good news is that you can use a modified version of this to stay 'on-value'. Once you've identified your core values (see previous chapter), it is quite simple, and involves asking yourself a few quick questions every time you make a decision or face a challenge. Next time this occurs, just ask yourself:

- What am I doing or thinking about?
- Is this task 'on-value'? (Am I acting according to my values?)
- If not, what would I do or think if I were 'on-value'?
- How can I bring myself back to my values?

This involves a degree of self-responsibility and accountability, so make sure you are honest with yourself.

64. There is nothing good or bad

Several decades of psychological research leaves us in no doubt that the way you think about things affects the way you feel and how you act. In simple terms, your thoughts will determine your mood and your actions.

To understand this better, keep a record of your thoughts, feelings and actions, in different contexts, over the course of the next week. Take a clean piece of paper, turn it sideways, and draw three lines down the page to create four columns. At the top of each column write the following headings: Situation, Thoughts, Feelings and Actions. When an interesting situation arises, record these details under each heading:

- Situation: where you were, who you were with, what you were doing.
- Thoughts: what was going through your mind.
- Feelings: how you would describe your mood (and you're allowed to record more than one emotion here).
- Actions: what you did, how you behaved or reacted.

After you've monitored your reactions for at least a week, set aside an hour to review what you've recorded and to reflect on what you could learn from the exercise.

You might also find it helpful to review this with a friend or someone who can be objective about the situations and your reactions to them. Ask this person how they might respond if they were in the same situation.

In time, you'll come to see that the nature and quality of your thoughts impact significantly on the extent to which a situation is or isn't distressing, and that there are different ways of thinking about things.

65. Trump negativity

There's a growing body of research that suggests happiness is not something that results from the number of positive events in your life, but rather the proportion of positive to negative events.

This could turn out to be quite important, as it would mean that our aim should not be to engage in as many positive events as possible, but rather to make sure positive activities outnumber negative ones.

One of the reasons this is worth considering is that we will always experience negative events in our lives – we'll never be able to totally eliminate them. What we *can* do is be mindful of the difficulties we're facing and try simply to focus more on those events and situations that are likely to engender positive emotions, if not maximise their occurrence as well.

To make the most of the proportional happiness principle:

- Try to reduce the number of negative events and experiences in your life.
- Try to increase the number of positive events and experiences in your life.
- Change the way you look at or think about negative events so they don't seem quite so bad or negative.
- Change the way you think about life generally so that you're more aware of, and more grateful for, all the positive things in your life. Don't take things for granted!

66. Practise 'happiness *kaizen*'

Recently I came across a definition of *kaizen*, a Japanese strategy for continuous improvement that can be applied in the workplace and is driven by both management and employees, the main principle of which is efficiency and the elimination of waste.

It struck me immediately that a similar philosophy would be just as relevant for individuals trying to achieve self-improvement and a better, happier life. So here's my slightly modified version of *kaizen*: 'Happiness *kaizen*' is a realistic, positive-psychology strategy for incremental, everyday improvement, driven by individuals and their significant others.

As a motto for living, I quite like the idea that you don't have to change everything all at once and you don't have to achieve all your goals right away; you can, instead, take small steps every day and eventually they'll accumulate and lead you towards a significant and positive change. You could apply this motto to your thoughts to start with – work toward eliminating one type of negative thought. For example, the 'I am not good enough' thought can be ignored or challenged each time it comes up. Alternatively, try and introduce consciously positive thoughts into your routine. An example might be to start your work day by visualising yourself dealing with the workload, and breaking the day down into small 'chunks' of different tasks.

67. Simplify your life

Not that long ago, in fact when I was about half way through writing this book, I went on a father-daughter camping weekend organised by some parents from my daughter's school. I had two days out of the city; beyond mobile-phone range; without television or other distractions; away from 'civilisation' – just a bunch of people spending a bunch of hours in a bunch of simple tents.

And that, my friends, is the tip . . . simplicity.

I gained an enormous amount of satisfaction and contentment from living a much simpler life, albeit for just a few short days. I'm not sure I'd want to live like this all the time, but what I do know is that I'd love to do it more often, because I can feel in my bones that it's good for me. And I bet it's good for you too.

Simplifying your life and your thinking can help streamline the process of implementing more happiness. If you happen to be someone who needs a variety of excitement, surprise, fun, laughter and camaraderie to satisfy themselves in a day, consider perhaps focussing on just one of these values, but making it count. Simply slowing down to enjoy something like a good meal can heighten your appreciation of it. Apply this policy to any aspect of your life with which you are not terribly happy right now, and it will be a load off your mind.

68. *Do* sweat the small stuff

It's true that many of us can get obsessed by minor detail and forget to see the bigger picture. This can be anything from a one-off hurtful remark made by a colleague (the big picture: normally the colleague is friendly and helpful) to fretting about some minor flaw in a project (the big picture: the rest of the project is exemplary).

In a way, this book is all about the small stuff, about dealing with problems in bite-sized chunks and creating little building blocks of achievement with which to make a happier you. But it's also about learning to recognise there are two very different approaches to 'small stuff' issues: the first, as described above, can result in obsessive and inaccurate thinking; the second, the type described here, can help you sort out the small things in your life, then use the knowledge acquired to tackle the bigger issues. In other words, sometimes it's good to think small.

I was reminded of this when playing Boggle with my wife. For those who don't know, Boggle involves shaking nine dice in a container; the dice have letters on each side, rather than numbers. The aim is to use the letters to create as many words as possible within two minutes. You gain more points for longer words and fewer for short words. There are two strategies: you can go for longer words and achieve more points (and look smarter), or you can accumulate small amounts of points quickly by making small words.

I went for the first strategy. I focussed on finding long, difficult words with which to impress my wife and score high. My wife, however, came up with a much longer list of much shorter words. I'll cut to the chase – she won comprehensively.

So what did I learn?

It's not always helpful to go for the grand statement, the thumping victory. Often change comes about by stacking up those small building blocks of achievement.

Think of a problem in your life right now, then break it down into three or four manageable parts. Write down each one on a separate piece of paper. Keep the piece of paper with the most pressing part of the problem in your wallet, and give yourself a deadline to deal with it. As you deal with each part of the problem, discard and replace the piece of paper in your wallet. When you have dealt with all the parts and discarded all the bits of paper, reward yourself.

A journey of a thousand miles begins with a single step.
Lao Tzu, c. 604–531 BC, Chinese philosopher

69. Think like an optimist

Some of us were born optimistic, or have been raised in ways that encouraged us to develop an optimistic mindset. But what of the rest of us, those who are more inclined towards pessimism?

The bad news for us pessimists is that research indicates we tend to get depressed more easily, and are therefore less happy for longer periods. The good news is we can change our mindset and turn ourselves into optimists, at least some of the time.

Optimism has been a key focus of the study of positive psychology. Martin Seligman, author of the classic text *Learned Optimism* and the more recent *Authentic Happiness*, defines an optimistic person as one who interprets setbacks in a particular way:

1. as temporary;
2. as specific to a particular situation;
3. due to external, not internal, reasons.

Here's an example. You are asked to complete a report for a project at work. You are given very little time to do it, and you do not have all the necessary information. You knock something together but you know it's not great. However, rather than beat yourself up, you explain the experience in the following way:

1. *Temporary:* 'I didn't do a great job this time, but normally my report-writing is excellent, and next time I will do better.'
2. *Specific:* 'I am very competent in my job overall; this is a slight glitch in just one small area.'

3. *External:* 'There was nothing wrong with my approach; I just wasn't briefed properly.'

Compare this to how the pessimist would deal with the same situation:

1. *Permanent:* 'This is terrible; it happens every time.'
2. *General:* 'My work generally has not been good; this is just one more indication of how poorly I am performing.'
3. *Internal:* 'It's all my fault; I should have worked harder.'

No prizes for guessing who leaves work at the end of the day in a happier state of mind.

As well as putting the best possible gloss on unfavourable events, optimists also take full advantage of favourable events, explaining them as permanent, general and internal (the exact opposite of how they explain unfavourable events). For example, if an optimist wins at tennis it is because he/she always plays well, usually wins and has superior skills to that of his/her opponent.

Next time you start explaining an unfavourable event in a pessimistic way, take a pause, get out a piece of paper and a pen, and try re-interpreting using the explanatory style of the optimist. Similarly, when something good happens, savour it for as long as possible, examine what you did to help create this event, and work out how you can use this experience in other areas of your life.

70. Be aware of your internal voice

Given the importance of your thinking in determining how you feel, and that the focus of this book is how to feel better, learning to be more aware of your thoughts is an essential part of boosting your happiness.

As often as possible, ask yourself the following questions:

- What thoughts are going through my mind?
- What am I saying to myself?
- What does this mean to me?
- What do I believe is going on here?

As you get better at identifying your thoughts you'll be far better positioned to take the next step, which is to challenge or question unhelpful negative thoughts, and to plant more optimistic ones that will help encourage positive emotions.

The unexamined life is not worth living.
Socrates, 470 BC–399 BC, Greek philosopher

71. Challenge your thoughts

Once you are able to flag your negative thoughts as they occur, you are on track to dismantling them. You won't always be able to stop negative thoughts forming – they are instinctive and automatic – however, the key is challenging them so that they can be re-interpreted in a more positive way, a skill you will find valuable throughout life.

Have you ever debated someone at a dinner party? Have you ever disagreed with someone in a meeting? Have you ever questioned your partner or a friend about something they did with which you didn't entirely agree? If you answer 'yes' to any of these questions, you already have the skills required to challenge others. Think of the process of challenging your own unhelpful thoughts as an internal debate – no different to questioning someone else.

If you've ever heard it said that talking to yourself is a sign of insanity then forget it – it's mostly not true. In fact, talking to yourself in a constructive way is a path to sanity and happiness.

As you become more aware of your thinking and you get better at identifying negative thoughts, remind yourself often that not all your thoughts will be helpful and realistic, and as such might not be helping you to be as happy as you could be. Challenge yourself on these thoughts just as you would challenge others whose opinion you didn't entirely agree with. Remember that the first thought is not always the correct thought.

72. Get a spam filter

Recently I read an amazing statistic – that almost two-thirds of all global email traffic is spam, and that the volume of spam to various devices such as mobile phones and online chat rooms is growing rapidly. As someone who often receives hundreds of emails each day, many of which are spam, it made me think how important it is to identify the spam quickly and delete it as soon as possible. Unsolicited email can place your computer at risk of viruses, and dealing with spam also soaks up valuable time and energy.

So then I got to thinking ... maybe automatic negative thoughts are the same?

If you allow these thoughts to linger, and start to believe them without appropriate consideration, you can put yourself at risk of a 'virus', which in human terms could be depression, anxiety or some other form of distress. Alternatively, you can build your own spam filter and learn how to delete these unwanted and unhelpful negative thoughts quickly and efficiently.

Easier said than done? I have compiled a list below of common negative thinking habits which we get into. Recognising them in your own thought-process is the first step to deleting them:

Overgeneralisation: Coming to a general conclusion based on a single event or one piece of evidence. If something bad happens once, you expect it to happen again and again. Such thoughts often include the words 'always' and 'never'.
Example: 'I forgot to finish that project on time. I never do things right.'
'He didn't want to go out with me. I'll always be lonely.'

Filtering: Concentrating on the negatives while ignoring the positives; ignoring important information that contradicts your (negative) view of the situation.

Example: 'I know my boss said most of my submission was great but he also said there were a number of mistakes that had to be corrected . . . he must think I'm really hopeless.'

All-or-nothing thinking: Thinking in black-and-white terms (eg things are right or wrong, good or bad); a tendency to view things at the extremes with no middle ground.

Example: 'I made so many mistakes.'
'If I can't do it perfectly I might as well not bother.'
'I won't be able to get all of this done, so I may as well not start it.'

Personalising: Taking responsibility for something that's not your fault. Thinking that what people say or do is some kind of reaction to you, or is in some way related to you.

Example: 'John's in a terrible mood. It must have been something I did.'
'It's obvious she doesn't like me, otherwise she would've said hello.'

Catastrophising: Overestimating the chances of disaster; expecting something unbearable or intolerable to happen.

Example: 'I'm going to make a fool of myself and people will laugh at me.'
'What if I haven't turned the iron off and the house burns down?'
'If I don't perform well, I'll get the sack.'

Emotional reasoning: Mistaking feelings for facts. Believing that negative things you feel about yourself are true because they feel true.
Example: 'I feel like a failure therefore I am a failure.'
'I feel ugly therefore I must be ugly.'
'I feel hopeless therefore my situation must be hopeless.'

Mind-reading: Making assumptions about other people's thoughts, feelings and behaviours without checking the evidence.
Example: 'John's talking to Molly so he must like her more than me.'
'I could tell he thought I was stupid in the interview.'

Fortune-telling: Anticipating an outcome and assuming your prediction is an established fact. These negative expectations can be self-fulfilling. Predicting what we would do on the basis of past behaviour may prevent the possibility of change.
Example: 'I've always been like this; I'll never be able to change.'
'It's not going to work out so there's not much point trying. This relationship is sure to fail.'

'Should' statements: Using 'should', 'ought', or 'must' statements can set up unrealistic expectations of yourself and others. It involves operating by rigid rules and not allowing for flexibility.
Example: 'I shouldn't get angry.'
'People should be nice to me all the time.'

Magnification/minimisation: The tendency to exaggerate the importance of negative information or experiences, while trivialising or reducing the significance of positive information or experiences.

Example: 'He noticed I spilled something on my shirt.'

'I know he said he will go out with me again,
but I bet he doesn't call.'

'Supporting my friend when her mother died still
doesn't make up for that time I got angry at her last year.'

73. Test the helpfulness of thoughts

Automatic negative thoughts are so-called because the impact they have is never good! In some way or other, they can lead to a negative mood state or can impact negatively on what you could or need to do to cope with a situation.

Negative moods such as stress, depression, anxiety and anger impact negatively on our coping resources. When we're distressed we just don't cope as well as when we're feeling more positive or calmer.

The simplest and easiest way to assess the helpfulness of a thought is by asking yourself the following questions:

- Is thinking this helping me feel better?
- Will this thought or way of thinking help me to solve this problem or overcome this difficulty?
- Am I predominately focussing on solutions or problems?
- Is my thinking energising or draining me?
- Will these thoughts increase or decrease the likelihood that I'll find an effective way out of this?

Any thoughts that are deemed to be counterproductive can happily be challenged, and this is a habit you will find builds over time.

74. Overcome worry

Worry is one of the more common enemies of happiness. Accordingly, managing and defeating worry is one of the more useful goals you can set yourself to achieve happiness. The good news is that worry is so common that psychologists have developed a range of effective tools for banishing (or at the very least minimising) unhelpful, ruminative and negative thoughts. Here are some tips you might like to try.

Tip 1 : Set aside a 'worry time'
Some people find it difficult to stop worrying. Anxious thoughts tend to intrude into their mind at all times, interfering with work or other activities. A useful way of dealing with this is to set aside a worry time. This can be, for example, half an hour just after work. At any other time, when an issue comes to mind, acknowledge to yourself that you need to think it through, and note that you will do so during your worry time. At the appointed time, think the issue through and try to use one of the approaches below. Before then, give yourself permission to put it out of your mind and to get on with the task at hand.

Tip 2 : Ask yourself, 'Is the problem solvable?'
Worrying partly functions as a problem-solving process: it alerts us to the possibility of something bad happening, and motivates us to come up with solutions to avoid bad outcomes. However, worriers often find it difficult to stop worrying because they attempt to solve problems that are not immediately solvable. So, during your worry time, the first thing you should ask yourself is whether you are agonising over a problem that is solvable or not.

Tip 3: Be realistic

Even if the problem is solvable, ensure your expectations are realistic. Worriers sometimes find it difficult to stop worrying because they keep trying to solve a problem to perfection. This is rarely possible. So, when you are trying to solve a problem, make sure that you aim to find a reasonable, rather than a perfect, solution. Worriers are very good at thinking of all the reasons why a solution would *not* work. They are not very good at thinking of any reason why a solution *would* work. So, when you are trying to problem-solve, make sure that you evaluate possible solutions in a more balanced way, not only paying attention to what may go wrong, but also to what may go right.

Tip 4: Be aware of unhelpful thoughts

One reason why problems and solutions seem so bad is that when we worry, we overestimate two things. First, we overestimate how likely it is that bad things will happen. Second, we overestimate how bad they would be, should they happen. Remind yourself of all the previous times when you worried about something that did not eventuate. Try to become more realistic in your assessment of the likely outcomes. This does *not* mean being unreasonably positive, just being more realistic.

Tip 5: Be your best friend

If you find it difficult to look at your negative thoughts objectively and challenge them to be more realistic, imagine that you are your own best friend. Think about all the negative things that you are thinking or saying to yourself: 'I'm such a loser. I never get anything right. I might as well give up now.' If your best friend was saying these things about themselves, what would you say to them? How would you challenge their negativity and self-criticism? Now remind yourself to be your own best friend and challenge your own negative thinking the same way.

Tip 6: Use your heart as well as your head

Sometimes problems cannot be resolved right away. In this instance, it is important to use 'emotion-focussed', rather than 'problem-focussed' coping techniques. In other words, accept circumstances as they are and put your efforts towards handling them.

Tip 7: Keep calm

Because worry tends to be so pervasive, worriers often experience chronic irritability, muscle tension, concentration difficulties, sleep problems, indecision and agitation (from being 'on edge' and unable to relax all the time). It is crucial, therefore, to make sure that you make a conscious effort to relax, even if for only a few minutes a day. There are a number of effective relaxation techniques described earlier in this book, and physical exercise is also one of the best remedies.

Tip 8: Be mindful

A relatively new technique that has been shown to be very useful to reduce worry and anxiety is mindfulness. It is, of course, not really new; it comes from very old Eastern meditative traditions. One of the main points of mindfulness is that you try to pay attention to the present moment. In order to worry, your attention needs to be focussed on the future, so if you successfully focus your attention on the present, you will find that your worrying stops. There are a number of good introductory books available on mindfulness that you may like to try (see Recommended resources on page 166), and I also give you an introduction on page 39.

Tip 9: Don't forget to sleep

Worry tends to interfere with sleep. In fact, lots of people do most of their worrying at night, while trying to fall asleep. This is of course a detrimental habit, and may lead you to lie awake for hours fretting about not being able to sleep! It is best to remind yourself to use bedtime as your time for relaxation and recuperation.

Tip 10: Don't think you have to do it all on your own!

Having a few friends to have fun with and to help you through difficult times is very important. Make sure you keep in touch with them and take time out. It is important to try and not let your concerns invade this time, so remind yourself of your designated 'worry-time', and pay attention to the present moment as much as possible.

> *When I look back on all these worries, I remember the story of the old man who said on his deathbed that he had a lot of trouble in his life, most of which had never happened.*
> Winston Churchill, 1874–1965, former British Prime Minister

75. Get into the game

Nothing is achieved on the sidelines; life is not a spectator sport. Read the following story and consider this theme:

> A group of animals and insects decided to organise a football game. The teams were organised according to size. All the big animals, including the bears, lions, elephants and giraffes, were on one team. Rabbits, squirrels, possums and insects formed the second team.
>
> The game got off to a predictable, one-sided start, and at the end of the first quarter the big animals were leading 56–0. By half-time, their lead had increased to 119–0. The small animals and insects had produced little by way of effective attack and their defence was not much to speak of either.
>
> As the second half started, the lion received the kick-off on the 25-metre line and was tackled on the 37-metre line. He immediately played the ball back to the bear who tried to charge up the middle, but was stopped straight away. On the next play the cheetah tried to use his pace to go around the outside but was brought down suddenly for a 1-metre loss of ground. The cheetah looked around to see who'd tackled him, and was surprised to see a centipede smiling back at him. 'Did you tackle me?' he asked the insect. 'This is the first time I've been tackled all day.'
>
> 'I sure did,' responded the brave little critter. 'I also tackled the lion and the bear!'
>
> One of the centipede's team-mates chimed in with, 'Well, that's great, but where were you during the first half when we were unable to make a single tackle?'
>
> The centipede replied, 'I was tying my laces'.

As you might have guessed, the centipede represents those people who are continually sitting on the sidelines. They intend to do something significant as soon as all the conditions are right and they're ready. They often expend considerable time and energy getting prepared to take action (like making sure their shoes are all tied), but when they finally get around to doing something, it's too late; the game's already lost!

While taking the time to prepare yourself for change is good, there is no point wasting energy on waiting for the right moment. When you have the momentum and inspiration to change, the best time to get started is the present.

Do you want to know who you are? Don't ask. Act!
Action will delineate and define you.
Thomas Jefferson, 1743–1826, 3rd President of the United States

76. Think again

Do you believe everything you read in the newspapers? Do you believe everything you see on television? I hope not!

Thoughts are not facts, and just because you think something, it doesn't mean it's true. As humans, we aren't perfect, and because we're not perfect we sometimes make mistakes in the way we think about things. Some of these thinking mistakes involve biases and prejudices, which are perfectly normal and okay – unless, that is, these biases are causing or contributing in some way to misery or unhappiness, and then that's not okay!

So next time you find yourself assuming something about an event or another person, ask yourself:

- What are the implications of believing what I believe?
- Is there a good reason for holding onto this belief? (Just because your mother or father or grandparents believed something isn't necessarily a good reason for maintaining a belief.)
- Is there any evidence for this belief?

Try this quick experiment. Open up the social pages of your local newspaper or a glossy magazine (the more sensational the publication the better, for this activity) and find a particularly outlandish headline. Read the article carefully and see how much information you can find that really supports the claim made in the headline. If possible, conduct additional research to determine the extent to which the claims made are true or not.

Now remember, in some instances the validity and reliability of your thoughts may be no different – so try the same approach to assessing the accuracy of your own thoughts.

Don't judge each day by the harvest you reap,
but by the seeds you plant.
Robert Louis Stevenson, 1850–1894, writer

77. Plant optimistic thoughts

In the same way as a farmer might stockpile feed for the dry season, it is worthwhile stockpiling optimistic thoughts so that you will have that resource to draw on when faced with a negative situation. Helpful thoughts, like a bountiful harvest, will be much easier to procure when times are good. Try these exercises and start to stockpile your positive thoughts. Think of as many positives as possible in:

- Your past
- Your present
- Your future
- Yourself
- Your world
- The other people in your life.

And then think about:

- What you can (rather than can't) do
- What you can (rather than can't) control
- Possibilities rather than limitations.

Keep this list handy as a tool to combating negativity when it occurs, and update and expand on it as often as possible.

78. Ask the question

Whenever you have a negative thought, stop and think, 'Is this helpful?'

We like to think of ourselves as purposeful and in charge, but the reality is that much of our thinking is fairly random. Even when we are focussed, our minds drift. Sometimes this is a pleasurable experience: we may think of our kids or of some fun activity we are planning for the weekend. Too often, though, our thoughts automatically veer in the opposite direction, and we find ourselves worrying or obsessing about things we have or haven't done, a hurtful comment from a friend, a setback at work or the irritating driver in front of us.

The odd negative thought is fine, and constructive critical thinking is very necessary for solving a particular kind of problem, but when we focus constantly on what is wrong rather than what is right in our lives, we squander our chance to be happy.

The question 'Is this helpful?' helps us put a spanner in the works of negative thinking. This is not about ignoring bad behaviour on the part of others or overlooking difficult problems that need to be addressed; it's about cutting back on the automatic negative thoughts that make us feel tired, grumpy and out of sorts. Here's a simple example.

A friend cancels an arrangement to see a movie. It's the third time she has done this in as many months. You have two options. The first is spending the evening going over the situation in your head, getting increasingly irritated with her behaviour and eventually going to bed in a grumpy state and sleeping badly. Your second option is to make a decision to question her about her behaviour when you next meet, then ring around to find another friend to invite to the movie – with luck, you'll have a great evening and by the end of it you have more or less forgotten the earlier slight.

At first it will take a bit of discipline to come up with alternative, more helpful thoughts to deal with the irritation and problems of daily life, but it's well worth the effort. And even if you can't avoid the negativity – perhaps the problem is too big or too intractable – you will learn to value the benefits associated with questioning how you think and react as opposed to following your gut instinct all the time.

If we can really understand the problem, the answer will come out of it, because the answer is not separate from the problem.
Jiddu Krishnamurti, 1895–1986, Indian religious philosopher

79. Stop the sky from falling – rationalise

We are most likely to get swept away with negative thoughts when we rely solely on our feelings to confirm them. If we psychologists always believed our gut feelings, our research would have led nowhere and uncovered no real answers. When you have a particularly anxious moment, step back and analyse the scene like a scientist. For example, imagine that your boss has found fault with some aspect of your work, and you have jumped to the conclusion that you are about to be sacked. Begin by looking for evidence. Ask yourself:

- What's the evidence for and against my thought?
- Am I focussing on the negatives and ignoring other information? (He did praise a few things as well.)
- Am I jumping to conclusions without looking at all the facts?

Then search for alternative explanations:

- Are there any other possible explanations? (Is he just in a grumpy mood?)
- Is there another way of looking at this?
- How would someone else think if they were in this situation?
- Am I being too inflexible in my thinking?

Put your thoughts into perspective:

- Is it as bad as I'm making out? What's the worst that could happen?

- How likely is it that the worst will happen? Even if it did happen, would it really be that bad? What could I do to get through it? (I'm good at what I do; the labour market favours employees at present so I'll get another job.)

Remember, the general consensus two millennia ago was that the Earth was flat. But it took a rational approach, and the gathering of all available evidence, to learn the reality. So make sure you do your research when a negative thought pulls you down.

80. Apply Pareto's Law

Although not originally conceived in the context of happiness studies, Pareto's Law states that for many events, 80 per cent of the outcomes result from 20 per cent of the causes. It has become a common rule of thumb in business to assume, for example, that 80 per cent of a business' sales will most likely come from 20 per cent of its clients. Accordingly, Pareto's Law has often been referred to as the 80/20 principle.

I think this law applies just as much to happiness, and for many of us, 80 per cent of our happiness derives from about 20 per cent of our activities or endeavours. And if this is a valid assumption, then the challenge is to get better at identifying the 20 per cent of what you do that makes you happy and to focus more on these things!

How can you do this? Keep a record of all the things you do over the course of the next week or two (no fewer than 3–4 days, to ensure you give yourself a chance to engage in a variety of activities and tasks), and next to your description of each activity simply record how much happiness you gain from each.

If you want to avoid overcomplicating the exercise, you can simply rate each item on a scale from zero to ten, where zero equals no happiness and ten equals the most happiness you can possibly imagine. If you're feeling a bit more adventurous, you could rate your activities on slightly different scales by scoring positive feelings such as pleasure, satisfaction, happiness, joy and fulfilment separately.

After you've done this for a few days (and again, the longer the period over which you do this, the more informative your ratings will be), and scored each and every entry, go back and review which activities were associated with the highest happiness ratings (you may be surprised). Then, quite simply, do more of these happiness-inducing activities. You could also look for themes and patterns and build these into your life as much as possible.

Most folks are about as happy as they make up their minds to be.
Abraham Lincoln, 1809–1865, 16th American President

Section Five

20 ways to plan and create a happy life

With the exception of a lucky few, most people are not blessed with intrinsic happiness; for most of us, happiness is not a beam of light that shines down from above, basking our lives in the soft glow of good fortune and happenstance. Rather, achieving happiness is more akin to fishing, in my mind. Those who take the time to thread their hook thoughtfully, and seek the kind of fish that swim in their particular river, are far more likely to find that they have a 'catch' at the end of the day. Happiness is something you can create right now, by adding some light and laughter to your life, and dealing effectively and wisely with adversity. It is also something that can be planned for, by putting in place strategies that will 'hook' a happy outcome or more positive mindset in the future. Significantly, we also need to find the time to put these strategies in place, and so this section will also deal with prioritisation and time management.

81. Set goals

Goal-setting can sound more intimidating than it really is. Having goals should be a comfort to you as well as a motivation for you. Follow these tips for successful goal-setting and watch your life change for the better:

1. Think about your life and what about it you would like to be different. Specify exactly what you would like to change. Imagine a happy future – what will you be doing then that is different to now? In particular, what will you be doing more of?

2. Write down exactly what you would like to achieve, both in the short term and the long term. Be as specific as possible. People who set specific goals are much more likely to succeed than those who set vague goals.

3. Record your goals in positive terms. Instead of stating your goal as 'To stop sleeping in', rephrase it by saying: 'My goal is to get up by 8:00 am every morning'. Again, focus on what you want more of in your life rather than what you want less of or what you want to get rid of.

4. Make sure your goals are realistic and achievable. If you set goals that are unrealistic then you might just find you're more likely to fail and be disappointed. To ensure you are being realistic, make sure you take into account all the relevant variables, including your financial situation, available time, emotional resources or other circumstances in life.

5. Divide your goal list up into short-term and long-term goals. Be realistic about how long it might take to achieve your goals. Often, a number of short-term goals need to be completed in order to

achieve longer-term goals. You can think of these as the rungs you need to climb to reach the top of a ladder. Where possible, set specific dates for completion of each goal.

6. Break down each goal into small steps. For example, if the goal is to find a new job, consider what steps you would have to take to achieve this. You might have to prepare a résumé (or update an old one), speak to an employment consultant, look in the newspaper and so on. Once again, set a date for the completion of each step.

7. When you achieve each step or the goal itself, acknowledge this by rewarding yourself. It is important to recognise your achievements. Each step you take is an achievement, and indicates that you are on your way to realising your goals.

You will be more likely to achieve your goals if they are clear, challenging but realistic, and rooted in your own values and priorities. Check also that what you need to do to achieve your goals is within your control. If they're dependent on someone else, you may struggle to achieve them through no fault of your own.

Lastly, reward yourself along the way; you needn't wait until you reach the very end.

82. Work and play using your strengths

We get pleasure from activities that emphasise our strengths and values, and from environments that allow our particular talents to be recognised and appreciated. If you are a person with a strong sense of beauty, you will feel much happier hand-making ceramics than mass-producing plastic widgets. If you have a belief in openness and opportunity, you will feel more comfortable in an organisation that has an open management structure than one that is rigidly hierarchical and secretive in its decision-making processes.

Sometimes when struggling at work, we need to take the time to pursue a favourite recreational activity that allows us to shine, in order to be reacquainted with our intrinsic strengths and values. Taking a long bushwalk could serve to remind you that your planning skills and capacity for endurance are top-level. Pulling off a dinner party for ten will highlight your organisational and networking talents. An afternoon of golf will reacquaint you with your superiority as a strategist and goal-setter. Spending time fostering particular talents and abilities is vital for building happiness. You can then apply this renewed confidence to tackling whatever adversities you are facing in your life, including those in the workplace.

Next time you're in a rut or feeling below par, go out and spend an afternoon, or even an hour, doing something that comes easily and gives you pleasure. Read 'Recognise your strengths' on page 19 and 'Clarify your values' on page 99 in order to focus on and think about the particular attributes that define you and drive your interests.

83. Visualise a happy you

Take a moment to imagine an aspect of your life in the future – this could be to do with your family, your career or just your lifestyle in general. Picture the things that have happened to you, and all you have accomplished. Imagine, in particular, that everything has gone as well as it possibly could have. You've worked hard, overcome hurdles and achieved the things you've always wanted.

Describe this life, focussing specifically on things you'd be doing that you're not doing now – that is, actual, observable behaviours that could be noticed by someone else, not just felt by you.

Visualisation is a technique that has been used successfully by athletes, leaders and entrepreneurs for years to help them achieve their goals. Visualising success actually primes you to perform the steps it takes to get there, and by taking positive action you're more likely to achieve positive outcomes.

84. Direct your own life story

During busy times, probably the last thing on your mind is your life goals; you are more likely to be concerned with the next meeting or exam you face, and consider life beyond that point as pure speculation! Remind yourself to take the time to invest in your own future. This can be as simple as discovering exactly what you hope your future might hold. The following are exercises that allow you to create your ideal life story, after which you can plot more specifically how to get there, or identify key themes and values explored in your models.

Letter from the future

Imagine yourself 20 or 30 years from now. You've had your ups and downs, but overall life's been pretty good and you're happy – satisfied and content with who you are and what you've made of your life.

Write a letter back to yourself explaining what has most effectively created and caused your happiness; reflect on your happiest moments and what the key ingredients were that led to you feeling good. Include as much detail as you can (such as specific events, interactions, people, thoughts and behaviours).

Lesson from the future

Picture yourself at the wise old age of 80 and imagine that this older version of you can speak to the here-and-now you. This 80-year-old you has experienced many challenges and joys, and achieved many victories. What are the most important lessons the future 80-year-old you would tell the here-and-now you? (Try and think of 2–3.)

Paint a picture

Don't worry if you don't feel you're very artistically talented, this exercise is not about creating a masterpiece. Instead, this activity is about having fun, being creative and approaching the challenge of defining and clarifying your purpose, direction and goals in a different way.

Imagine a scene 10, 20 or 30 years from now, in which you are wondrously happy. What does this look like? Where are you? What are you doing? Who are you with?

Create a collage

Gather up some old books or magazines. Spend some time looking through the pages of these books and magazines and cut out any images that resonate with you, or that you feel represent the life you'd like to live and the goals you'd like to achieve. Put these images together in any way you like, to form a collage of the things you feel capture an experience or feeling that is consistent with you, your happy life, your purpose, direction and values. Feel free to add words, drawings or anything that would enhance the image you're trying to create – a great and inspirational life.

> *Destiny is not a matter of chance, it is a matter of choice; it is not a thing to be waited for, it is a thing to be achieved.*
> William Jennings Bryan, 1860–1925, American politician and orator

85. Create your ideal 'happiness pie'

You've probably heard the saying that when something's simple it's a 'piece of cake'. Well, I think life should be simple, but more than a *piece* of cake – I think it should be a whole pie.

For those of you who've forgotten your high-school maths, a pie chart is essentially a circle with lines radiating out from the centre, dividing the 'pie' into 'pieces' depending on the relative size of the portions to the whole. You can plot your own happiness in the same way by creating a 'happiness pie'. This simple exercise is about reviewing openly and honestly where your life's at now, and where you'd like it to be. So, with this in mind, carry out the following tasks:

1. Ask yourself 'What's my life like now?' On what activities or in which pursuits do you spend your time?
2. List all the various 'activity domains' in your life. Estimate the percentage of your time you spend in each domain, and illustrate this in a pie chart. (Your pie chart might include large segments for social life and spirituality, smaller pieces for health, recreation and education, and tiny slivers for finance and holidaying. Someone else's may look entirely different.)
4. Now ask yourself 'What would I like my ideal life to look like?' Repeat steps 2 and 3, then compare the differences.

Give some thought to how you can start moving from where your life is now towards your ideal!

86. Make a substitution

Okay, this one's short and sharp, but it's also profound and potentially life-changing.

Write down one thing in your life (and it doesn't necessarily have to be a big thing) that makes you unhappy and that you would like to change or stop right now. You could commit to stopping smoking, drinking less, eating less fatty foods or arguing less with someone you love. Write down exactly when and how you're going to effect this change.

Then, write down one thing (and again, it might only be a small thing) that you could start doing or do more of and that would, in some way, improve the quality of your life. You might decide to eat more fruit, walk or exercise more, read more fiction, practise relaxation or meditation, be more grateful and appreciative, tell others you love them or simply put time into having fun and laughing.

Start with this small, positive substitution; a clear, defined goal. This will work particularly well if you choose a new activity that will easily fit into the time that the old one took up. For example, you may choose to go for a walk instead of eating dessert; read a book instead of watching television. Once you find you have successfully altered your behaviour, you can try this exercise again and again. It is particularly helpful as a jumping-off point when you feel your life needs refreshing.

87. Eulogise your ideal life

Think of 3–5 people you admire most in the world. They could be writers, politicians, next-door neighbours, family, friends or your Year 6 teacher.

Reflect on what you admire most about these people – what do they do that differentiates them from others? How do they behave that makes them stand out from the crowd? What attributes or characteristics do they display that you'd like to emulate?

Describe each person's admirable qualities in no more than 10 words and then consider what you might be able to do to engage in this type of behaviour yourself. How would you like to be remembered? What would you like your legacy to be?

Imagine life after you've gone (yes, the world will keep turning!). Imagine your family and friends sitting around one day discussing you and your life. What would you most like them to say? What would you most like to hear them reminisce about? On what achievements would you most like to hear them reflect?

Are you living a life that would lead to this right now? If you are, then give yourself a hearty pat on the back. If you're not, then work out what you need to do and change to live a life that will lead to you being remembered in a positive way.

A variation on this exercise is to imagine yourself 20 or 30 years from now. You're reminiscing and reflecting on your life. You recognise your achievements and are pleased with some successes, but …

- What would your 'buts' be?
- What regrets do you think you'd have about the way you're living your life now?
- What are you going to do about it *now*?

Our experience truly is the sum of all our previous behaviours. Therefore you have the opportunity now, today, to build the framework for future and lasting happiness.

> *Our care should not be to have lived long as to have lived enough.*
> Lucius Annaeus Seneca, c. 4 BC–65 AD, Roman philosopher

88. Maximise happiness productivity

One day an expert on time management was speaking to a group of business students and, to drive home a point, he decided to conduct a demonstration. As he stood in front of the group of over-achievers he said, 'Okay, time for a quiz.'

He pulled out a very large, wide-mouthed jar and set it on a table in front of him. Then he produced about a dozen fist-sized rocks and carefully placed them, one at a time, into the jar.

When the jar was filled to the top and no more rocks could fit inside, he asked, 'Is this jar full?' Everyone in the class said yes.

He said, 'Really?' then reached under the table and pulled out a bucket of gravel. He poured some gravel in and shook the jar, causing pieces of gravel to work themselves down into the spaces between the big rocks. Then he smiled and asked the group once more, 'Is the jar full?'

By this time the class was on to him. 'Probably not!' was the answer.

'Good!' he replied. Then he reached under the table and brought out a bucket of sand. He poured the sand into the spaces left between the rocks and the gravel. Again he asked, 'Is the jar full?' 'No!' the class shouted.

Again he said, 'Good!' Then he took a jug of water and began to pour it in until the jar was filled to the brim. Again he asked, 'Is the jar full?'

Many in the class said 'Yes'. Others weren't so sure, and they smiled as he took a salt shaker and emptied it into the jar as well.

Then he looked up at the class and asked, 'What is the point of this demonstration?'

One eager beaver raised his hand and said, 'The point is, no matter how full your schedule is, if you try really hard, you can always fit something more into it.'

'No,' the speaker replied. 'That lesson could be drawn from this, but that's not the point I wish to make. The truth this demonstration teaches us is that if you don't put the big rocks in first, you won't get them in at all.'

What are the big rocks in your life? Do they include a project you want to accomplish? Spending more time with loved ones? Education? Your faith, your fitness, your finances, a cause?

Whatever they may be, know what your own big rocks are, and remember to put them in first, or you won't get them in at all.

89. Put yourself first

If you've ever flown in an aeroplane and listened to the safety instructions, you might remember that during the flight attendants' safety demonstration, they typically say something along the lines of: 'If oxygen is needed a mask will drop down from the ceiling. Be sure to put your own mask on first and then, if you're travelling with children, help them with theirs.'

Now, as a parent I imagine this would be very difficult to do. For most parents their first thought would probably be about how to help their child. There is, though, an important lesson we can learn from this.

We can't possibly look after others until we've looked after ourselves. I can't be a good husband or father or employer or friend if I'm tired and miserable! In contrast, I'll be a much better spouse and parent if I'm happy and healthy.

But many of us get this wrong because we think taking care of ourselves is selfish. Well, selfishness is not necessarily a good thing, but it shouldn't in any way be confused with appropriate self-care. Appropriate self-care is good for us and for all the people around us.

Set aside some time on a regular basis to take care of your physical and psychological needs. Build this into your life so it doesn't get forgotten or sacrificed for what might appear to be more important matters.

Example is not the main thing in influencing others. It is the only thing.
Albert Schweitzer, 1875–1965, Alsatian theologian, musician and medical missionary

90. Plan mini-breaks

Quickly answer the following question: If you had to rate, between zero and ten, the extent to which you enjoyed Friday afternoons versus Sunday evenings, which would you rate higher?

If you're lucky enough to be extremely happy at work and love what you do, you'll probably rate your Sunday evenings high because you can't wait to get back to work on Monday morning. If, however, you're like many of the overly busy people for whom this book was written, then you'll probably rate your Friday afternoons much higher than your Sunday evenings, as you spend the week desperately hanging out for the weekend. This, my friends, is not a good situation to be in – living your life madly trying to get through the week to enjoy the weekend.

There is, however, a quick and simple solution to this, and it is contained in the answer to the following question: What do you enjoy most about weekends and holidays, and how can you do this more regularly in your normal working week?

If you can find the core elements of what it is you enjoy about your days off from work, then there's a pretty good chance you might be able to incorporate at least some of these into your Monday to Friday routine.

Could you, for example, see your friends more during the working week for a quick coffee, lunch or for a drink after work? Could you engage in one of your hobbies before or after work, or even, when appropriate, during a lunch break? Could you incorporate relaxation, meditation or exercise into your lunch break or some other part of your day? The working week need not be a life sentence, so work at bringing some balance back to your agenda.

91. Prioritise tasks

For many people, stress is caused or aggravated by time pressure – the feeling that there is too much to do in any one day or week. Many argue that learning to manage your time is one of the most helpful ways to reduce stress, but I only partly agree with this, and that's because time can't really be managed.

Each and every one of us has the same amount of time in which to live our lives and do what we want to do. What differentiates the really happy and successful people from others is not that they have more time, but that they're markedly better at focussing on the right things: those things that really are important (as opposed to those which merely seem important or urgent at the time).

Effective time-management really involves effectively prioritising and planning your activities, as well as considering creative ways to get more out of your day. Although this in itself takes time, it is important because it will save you time and reduces stress in the long term. If you think that you could benefit from improving the way you prioritise and organise those things in your life that matter, consider the following tips.

List all of the tasks you think you need to do in one day (or week or month, depending on how good you are at thinking and planning ahead). Then label the tasks as follows, according to how important and urgent they are:

- A tasks – These are tasks that are both important and need to be done immediately, such as crises and projects driven by deadlines.

- B tasks – These are tasks that are important but do not necessarily need to be done immediately, such as preparation, research, planning, healthy living activities and recreational pursuits.

- C tasks – These are tasks that need to be done someday but are not that important right now. For example, some phone calls, errands and longer-term projects that would be nice to complete but which won't cause any major disturbance if they're not ever addressed.

- D tasks – All those tasks that are not important or urgent and are effectively time-wasters, such as watching television or surfing the internet.

The key to effective time, or should I say, priority-management is to dedicate as much time as possible to A and B tasks, while minimising the time you spend on C and, especially, D tasks. Being realistic, you will always spend some time engaging in C and D tasks, and that's okay, but if you're looking for ways to be more productive, more efficient, happier and more successful then, unless you can find a way to increase the number of hours in a day or the number of days in a week, your next best option is to spend the time that you do have on those activities that will provide the best return on investment, from both a financial and psychological wellbeing perspective.

92. Refine your workload

In addition to the priority-management tips just outlined, if you also think you could benefit from saving time, consider the following strategies when looking at your task workload.

Ask yourself, 'Does this task really have to be done today?' If tasks are not essential, then cross them off your list or remove them from your diary or calendar, but – and this is an important consideration – make sure you don't remove items just because they are boring or unpleasant.

Ask yourself, 'Is there a more efficient way to do this task?' For example, could you write an email instead of making a lengthy phone call? Could someone else do the task for you? Could some tasks be shared with others?

If you are worried that someone else would not do the task as well as you, ask yourself, 'How likely is it that it won't be done properly?' and 'What would really happen if the other person didn't do it correctly or didn't do it exactly the same way I would do it?'

Identify and address reasons for procrastinating. If you don't like doing a particular task, set specific goals for completing it (eg spend 2 hours on the task each day) and use strategies such as rewarding yourself to provide motivation for completion.

If you don't know how to go about beginning a task, break the task into smaller sections and set dates for the completion of each section. Then complete one section at a time.

If you are worried about the finished product not being perfect, ask yourself, 'Is it better to do something reasonably than not at all?'

Be assertive with others and practise saying 'no' to their requests if the tasks they're asking you to do are not essential or important. Ask yourself,

'How likely is it that these people will be angry or unhappy just because I do not have time to do something for them?'

The next step is to schedule time for the tasks you have listed. Draw up a daily timetable, including as much detail as possible. For example:

- Start by scheduling an appointment for those tasks that have to be completed at a specific time (eg attending a meeting).
- For deadline-driven tasks, realistically estimate how long the task will take, and work backwards from the deadline to determine when it needs to be started so that it is completed on time. If you're constantly struggling to meet deadlines, then it may well be that you're underestimating the time it takes to complete projects and that you're simply not being realistic. If needs be, intentionally over-estimate the time required to complete tasks.
- Allocate realistic deadlines to the other tasks, alternating the really important tasks with something a bit less strenuous and more relaxing.
- Plan and factor in time for interruptions and tasks that take longer than expected by sandwiching large, important tasks between smaller, less urgent ones.
- Stick to your agenda. Do the task you set out to do and don't be distracted by other tasks that arise. Instead, schedule time to do these tasks later and if necessary, assertively tell other people that their requests will need to wait.
- Remember to schedule rewards for yourself, which may include rests or enjoyable tasks after particularly difficult jobs.

93. Stop waiting for happiness

Do you want your tombstone to read, 'Here lies "so and so", who was going to be happy tomorrow'?

If not, then you should seriously consider what you're doing now and what you might need to do to be happy right now – this very moment!

One of the greatest obstacles to happiness is what I've come to refer to as 'the tyranny of when.' How many of you have ever said, at some time or other, 'I'll be happy when I have more money/a bigger house/ a faster car/the latest gadget.'

If you have then you're perfectly normal, because we all do this at times, but nevertheless you're jeopardising your happiness. Why? Because although material possessions are not bad, they won't ever lead to anything more than a short-term, superficial form of positive emotion (not 'real' happiness). And further, happiness can only ever be experienced at one point in time – and that's the here and now!

So save money and work for the things you want if that's something that you enjoy, but don't expect material objects to bring you deep and meaningful positive emotions. Research shows time and time again that once we reach a base level of prosperity – when our needs for food and shelter are met – the addition of money and material goods does not affect our personal happiness one bit. Real and authentic happiness will only ever come from optimistic thoughts and meaningful and positive relationships.

Don't wait until all aspects of your life are perfectly in order to enjoy happiness. Why should you? If you waited until all the traffic lights between your home and your destination were green before leaving in the morning, you'd never get out the front door.

94. Be curious about the world

Studies have shown that there are a number of personality traits associated with higher levels of happiness, and one of the more interesting is curiosity. Positive psychologists divide curiosity into two parts (as you may have noticed, psychologists can't resist a category!): exploration (the tendency to seek out new and challenging situations), and absorption (the tendency to become fully engaged in these interesting situations).

Exploration in particular is associated with higher levels of happiness. It could be that when we do something new, our minds become more focussed, more engaged. We lose ourselves in novelty, forcing our niggling worries to take a backseat.

Spontaneity is curiosity's driver. If your life is too structured or rigid, you won't create room to pursue new and different tasks and interests. Happy people look for opportunities to be flexible, and build creativity into their routine. Even though it sounds like a contradiction in terms, happy people plan for spontaneity.

You can do this by consciously setting aside a block of 'new' time each week or month to pursue something new, such as:

- Building a new friendship by inviting a colleague or acquaintance for coffee
- Taking up a sport
- Signing up for a course
- Taking on a new challenge at work
- Travelling somewhere different
- Joining a club

- Volunteering in an unfamiliar area or one that
  allows you to use undeveloped skills.

Your experience of the world will expand, your skills in your chosen area will improve, your knowledge of the world will deepen, and, yes, you'll make yourself happier.

> *Sail away from the safe harbour. Catch the trade winds in your sails. Explore. Dream. Discover.*
> Mark Twain, 1835–1910, American writer

95. Lighten up

We like to think our minds are in charge and that our thoughts direct our behaviour, but this is not always the case. Studies have shown over and over again that what we do with our bodies can determine how we feel and think. For example, if you smile, your mood improves, even if you don't feel particularly happy to begin with. Yes, it's true. Researchers conducted an experiment with participants who were forced to smile because they were asked to hold a pen between their teeth (try it yourself). At the end of the exercise, the participants with the pens were found to feel measurably happier than the participants in the control group (those without pens).

Anyone who has been around children knows how quickly a bad mood can be improved by engaging the child in some simple, fun activity such as dancing, throwing a ball or having a run in the park. The good news is that we adults can lighten up our mood by doing things that are silly, easy, frivolous and fun. Here are some suggestions:

- Put on some music and have a dance, or go out on a dancing date
- Join a choir or sing at a karaoke bar with a friend
- Listen to live music
- Wear clothes a few shades brighter than normal
- Practise laughing out loud
- Play backyard cricket
- Share a joke with a friend
- Go walking on a really windy day
- Go bodysurfing
- Go to the park and have a go on the swings.

Make a point of having fun at least once a day. If you find you are letting it slip, ask yourself, seriously, how many more days are you prepared to lose in sober concentration?

Don't take life too seriously or you'll never get out of it alive.

Elbert Hubbard, 1856–1915, American writer

96. Deal with adversity

One morning I took my young son for a play in the park on the way to preschool, where there were some kids' toys lying around for general use. My son started playing with a plastic truck and as he prepared to move it along some imaginary path he had planned in his mind, it soon became apparent that the other toys lying around were in his way.

As a rational adult my first reaction was to think about picking up the toys that were in the way so he could move the truck along his ideal trajectory, but my son didn't even think of this. Instead, he simply picked up the truck, carried it over the other toys, and continued along his merry way.

It got me thinking about what we adults often do (or don't do) when things get in the way of our goals or our happiness. Do you focus too much on obstacles and what you think you need to do to remove them? Do you allow road blocks to distract your attention from the ultimate goal (eg happiness)? Because focussing on an obstacle – even if we think we're trying to overcome it – is still focussing on an obstacle!

What would happen if we, like my son, simply stayed focussed on what we wanted to achieve, despite the hurdles, obstacles and challenges that frequently get in our way? Think about it – I suspect we might be far more successful and focussed on our positive outcomes and ultimately, I suspect we'd experience far more happiness. Ask the right questions during difficult times:

- What's the best thing about this situation?
- What positives can I take from this?
- What can I learn from this situation?

- How can I be a better person as a result of this?
- In ten years' time will this really matter?
- How bad is this compared to the worst events in the world?

Consider the following:

- 3 billion people live on less than $2 a day
- 30 000 children die daily of preventable diseases
- 6 million children die annually from malnourishment
- 113 million children do not have the chance to go to school.

How bad does it seem now? Ask yourself how you can use your strengths to get through difficult times. Are you making the most of the resources available to you?

> *We may need to solve problems not by removing the cause but by designing the way forward even if the cause remains in place.*
> Edward de Bono, born 1933, English authority on creative thinking

97. Take action to maintain happiness

Another way to maintain your happiness is to face up to the simple reality that no matter who you are, or what your situation is, no matter how well you practise these strategies and no matter how hard you try to be happy, we will all, at some time or another, have to face up to problems and difficulties and overcome obstacles. Accepting this in advance, making it part of how you live your life, will allow you to better deal with problems when they arrive.

When faced with difficulties, we all have a number of choices in terms of how we deal with them. Remember, it's not the problem that does the damage but what we do (or don't do) about it. Accordingly, we owe it to ourselves, and to those we love, to deal with these problems and then to try to move on.

As humans, we'll experience a range of emotions (both positive and negative) throughout our lives. Happiness is not just about enjoying the good times (although this is an important part of happiness) but also about working through difficulties.

Happy people tend to face these challenges more effectively. They're more resilient, and resilience breeds happiness. Next time you're experiencing difficulties, facing adversity or struggling with challenges, try the following resilience tips which have been tested and recommended.

- Use your support network. Happy and resilient people don't necessarily cope with everything on their own, but rather they reach out and ask for help.
- When and where appropriate, use humour and laughter to see things differently and to remain positive.

- By all means, learn from your experiences, but don't dwell on the past – especially on things that can't be changed.
- Practise helpful thinking strategies and do whatever you can to remain hopeful and optimistic about the future.
- Don't catastrophise but instead try to keep things in perspective.
- Look after your physical health and make sure you get plenty of sleep and rest.
- Accept the reality that the world is not perfect, and accept the inevitability of change.
- Don't lose sight of your purpose, direction and goals, nor of your dreams.
- Don't stop working towards your goals.
- Try to learn more about yourself and focus on the positives within yourself and the world.

Remember, happiness is not something you should only experience when things are going well. If you practise these resilience strategies then you can also experience happiness during times of difficulty.

The ultimate measure of a man is not where he stands in moments of comfort and convenience but where he stands at times of challenge and controversy.
Martin Luther King, 1929–1968, American civil rights activist

98. Be prepared for setbacks

Building on the aforementioned resilience tips, these additional tips are designed to help you overcome setbacks more easily and to recover more effectively.

- Have a plan – don't wait until a setback hits before you consider what to do about it. Be prepared and have a list of things to do (and not to do). This way, you will have done half the work beforehand and you won't have to come up with lots of ideas during what could be a difficult period.
- Get in early – the sooner you act, the sooner you'll overcome your setback, and the less likely your problems will develop and grow. Setbacks are easier to deal with if you catch them early. To do this, look out for early-warning signs and then act quickly.
- Remind yourself that everyone has setbacks, and although they are not pleasant, they are pretty normal. Accordingly, don't be too hard on yourself, but instead assure yourself that you will get through this and be all the stronger for your efforts.
- Review what has helped you in the past – go back and consider the changes you've made that have been most helpful. Do you need to look at your thinking, your behaviour or your communication skills? Are you looking after yourself and sleeping well? If you've stopped using any of the happiness strategies that had previously helped you, try to get started again and re-focus on what has helped you in the past.

• Remind yourself of the gains you've made rather than focussing unhelpfully on the temporary setback.

Success is the ability to go from one failure to another with no loss of enthusiasm.
Winston Churchill, 1874–1965, former British Prime Minister

99. Handle your problems

No matter what the problem is you're facing, there will invariably be a solution – sometimes you just have to look hard for it. Try the following strategies:

- *Define the problem:* What's going on here? Be as specific, realistic and clear as possible, and break down big problems into smaller ones.
- *Brainstorm potential solutions for the problem:* Generate as many solutions as you can think of – let your imagination run wild.
- *Assess your potential solutions:* Examine the advantages and disadvantages (pros and cons) of each possible solution, and choose one solution that you think will work best for you.
- *Generate an action plan:* Now that you've chosen an effective solution, work out how you can put this plan into action. What do you need to do to make this plan work? Once again, be as specific as possible.
- *Put the plan into action:* Try it out. Do it. If you need to, rehearse it in your mind first, or discuss it with a friend beforehand.
- *Evaluate the outcome:* Did it work? If not, can you modify the plan? If not, try and define the problem again or alternatively, consider other potential solutions.

100. Live like a five-year-old

One day, during the writing of this book, I returned home from work and asked my son (who was five years old at the time), 'What did you do today?'

He responded with something along the lines of, 'I played in the park with Henry [his best mate] and Max.'

Wanting to keep the conversation going longer than six seconds, I asked, 'Did you have fun?'

He immediately responded, 'Why wouldn't I, Dad?' with a hint of disbelief that I would even ask such a question.

Surprised by the simplicity of his response, I laughed. Unsure about my reaction he reiterated, 'Well, why wouldn't I have fun, Dad?'

Like many young children, my son has a fantastic ability to have fun, wherever he is – in fact, he approaches most situations as opportunities to have fun. He expects each and every day to be a fun, happy one. What a wonderful way to approach life!

Now I know we (that's us adults) have responsibilities and chores, but I couldn't help but wonder what it would be like if we all approached each day with an attitude similar to that of my son's. Not, 'Will I have fun?' but 'Why wouldn't I have fun?'

So act like a five-year-old sometimes. Adults have an amazing ability to overcomplicate things, and often we imagine life is far more difficult than it needs to be. Being happy doesn't result from solving the world's problems, it is a state of mind with which you confront the world's problems. Why don't you try it out and see what happens?

Finally ...

Contemplate or meditate on this slightly modified version of the Serenity Prayer:

Change what you can change
Accept what you can't change
And learn to be wise enough to know the difference.

Recommended resources

Buckingham, Marcus, *Go Put Your Strengths to Work*, Simon & Schuster, 2007

Emmons, Robert, *Thanks: How the new science of gratitude can make you happier*, Houghton Mifflin Company, New York, 2007

Frisch, Michael B., *Quality of Life Therapy*, John Wiley & Sons, New Jersey, 2005

His Holiness the Dalai Lama (translated by Howard Cutler), *The Art of Happiness*, Hodder, Sydney, 1998

Kabat-Zinn, J., *Wherever you go, there you are: Mindfulness Meditation in Everyday Life*, Hyperion Books, New York, 1995

Lundin, Stephen C., Paul, Harry and Christensen, John, *Fish!*, Charthouse, 1998

Lyubomirsky, Sonia, *The how of happiness – A scientific approach to getting the life you want*, Penguin Press, New York, 2008

Post, Stephen and Neimark, Jill, *Why Good Things Happen to Good People*, Broadway Books, New York, 2007

Seligman, Martin, *Authentic Happiness,* Random House, Sydney, 2002

—*Learned Optimism,* Random House, Sydney, 1991

Thich Nhat Hanh, *Peace is Every Step: The Path of Mindfulness in Everyday Life*, Bantam, New York, 1992

www.authentichappiness.org
www.drhappy.com.au
www.eightprinciples.com
www.gimundo.com
www.thehappinessinstitute.com
www.viastrengths.org

Acknowledgements

I'm extremely grateful to Julie Gibbs and Ingrid Ohlsson at Penguin for having faith in this book, and to Janet Manley and Virginia Birch for their expertise in helping me shape it into what you now have before you.

And an enormous thanks to all the members of The Happiness Institute community. Through your attendance at our seminars, courses and coaching, via your emails and suggestions, and as a result of your contributions to my web-blog, you have, directly and indirectly, knowingly and unknowingly, assisted with the development of my ideas and with the formulation of this book – for that, again, I'm grateful.

Index

ALSO FROM PENGUIN

A New Earth
Eckhart Tolle

Illuminating, enlightening, and uplifting, *A New Earth* is a profoundly spiritual guide to creating a better way of living and a better world to live in. Building on the astonishing success of *The Power of Now*, Eckhart Tolle presents readers with an honest look at the current state of humanity: he implores us to see and accept that this state, which is based on an erroneous identification with the egoic mind, is one of dangerous insanity.

Tolle tells us there is good news, however. There is an alternative to this potentially dire situation. Humanity now, perhaps more than in any previous time, has an opportunity to create a new, saner, more loving world. This will involve a radical inner leap from the current egoic consciousness to an entirely new one.

In illuminating the nature of this shift in consciousness, Tolle describes in detail how our current ego-based state of consciousness operates. Then gently, and in very practical terms, he leads us into this new consciousness. We will come to experience who we truly are – which is something infinitely greater than anything we currently think we are – and learn to live and breathe freely.

What's Happening to Our Girls?
Maggie Hamilton

Why are girls as young as five years old concerned about their looks and addicted to shopping?

Why are they having sex and binge-drinking so young, responding to chat-room predators, and bullying their peers via email and text messages?

Why are depression, cutting and eating disorders on the rise, and why, with so much choice, do so many just want to marry young and have babies?

In a few short years our girls have become vulnerable – not just teen girls, but also young girls and baby girls. They are being forced to grow up faster than ever before. What a twelve-year-old girl experienced at seven is not what a seven-year-old girl is now struggling with. Many of the guidelines we offer girls no longer apply, or are contradicted by messages from media and advertising telling girls how to look, think, behave and feel.

Over two years Maggie Hamilton interviewed girls, teachers, school counsellors, psychologists, and law enforcement and medical personnel to get an insider's view on what girls are experiencing at present, from birth to the teenage years.

Informed, revealing, compassionate and at times shocking, *What's Happening to Our Girls?* is a book for parents and all those who want to better understand and support girls.